THE GOLD GUIDES

SAN FRANCISCO

A COMPLETE GUIDE FOR VISITING THE CITY

Text by
Robert Fitzgerald

Photographs by
Andrea Pistolesi

CONTENTS

Introduction 3	
Section One	
DOWNTOWN 7	
Union Square 8	
Theatres 15	
Shopping 16	
Financial District 18	
Civic Center 30	
Section Two	
CHINATOWN	
AND NORTH BEACH 37	
Chinatown 38	
North Beach 44	
Telegraph Hill 49	
Russian Hill 52	
Nob Hill 54	
Section Three	
SOUTH OF MARKET	
AND THE MISSION 61	
South of Market 62	
South Park 68	
The Mission 69	
Potrero Hill District 73	
Section Four	
THE HAIGHT AND THE CASTRO .74	
Twin Peaks 75	

Noe Valley 76
The Haight 76
The Castro 77
Section Five
THE WATERFRONT 79
The Presidio 80
Golden Gate Bridge 84
The Marina 89
Fort Mason and
  Northern Waterfront 91
Fisherman's Wharf 92
The Embarcadero 104
Section Six
PACIFIC HEIGHTS AND
  CENTRAL NEIGHBORHOODS ..107
Pacific Heights and
  Victorian Houses 108
Japantown 112
Section Seven
GOLDEN GATE PARK
  AND THE WEST 115
Golden Gate Park 116

OTHER 121
EASY TRIPS
  FROM SAN FRANCISCO 123
INDEX 128

Project and editorial conception: Casa Editrice Bonechi.
Publication Manager: Monica Bonechi. *Picture research:* Monica Bonechi
Graphic design and make-up: Serena De Leonardis, Manuela Ranfagni.
Cover: Manuela Ranfagni. *Editing:* Anna Baldini, Giovannella Masini. *Maps:* Daniela Mariani

Text by Robert Fitzgerald
Pages 63 (Sony Metreon), 117 (M.H. de Young Museum), 118 (Asian Art Museum), 122
(3-Com and Pacific Bell Parks): *texts by* Cristiana Pace. *Page 127: text by* Richard Dunbar

© Copyright by Casa Editrice Bonechi - Florence - Italy
E-mail: bonechi@bonechi.it - Internet: www.bonechi.it

Collective work. All rights reserved. No part of this publication may be reproduced, or transmitted in any form or by any means, whether electronic, chemical, or mechanical, photocopying, or otherwise (including cinema, television, and any information storage and retrieval system) without the express written permission of the publisher. The cover and layout of this publication are the work of Casa Editrice Bonechi graphic artists and as such are protected by international copyright.
Printed in Italy by Centro Stampa Editoriale Bonechi.

Photographs from the archives of Casa Editrice Bonechi *taken by*
Andrea Pistolesi.

Fine Arts Museums of San Francisco: *page 117.* Courtesy of the Golden Gate National Recreation Area (Don Denevi Photographic Collection): *pages 100 above and below right, 101 left (above and center) and right (below), 102, 103.* Photo kindly supplied by Ken Glaser: *pages 53, 124 center.*
Andrew Mc Kinney: *page 121.* Realy Easy Star: *pages 9 -3rd photo from top to bottom (ph. Claudio Rizzi), 21 below (ph. Marco Passanisi), 26 below left (ph. Claudio Rizzi).*
SFMOMA Permanent Collection: *pages 65, 66.* Wells Fargo Bank: *pages 24,25.*

ISBN 978-88-8029-894-6

* * *

INTRODUCTION

America's favorite city, San Francisco sits perched above one of the world's most beautiful junctures of land and sea.

Surrounded on three sides by water, San Francisco is foremost a city of exquisite views. First-time visitors and age-old residents alike are awed every day by the awesome sight of the sun rising over San Francisco Bay and the twilight fog enveloping the Golden Gate Bridge and the surrounding hills. Around each corner and at the crest of every hill, San Francisco's natural beauty sets it apart from all of the other great cities of the world.

For all of its geographical splendor, however, what makes San Francisco unique is the people who live there. Throughout the city's history, San Francisco has been defined by the distinctive and unusual personalities of those who venture to settle there.

San Francisco sits at the edge of the Western

The logo of the Fisherman's Wharf, and some characteristic pictures of San Francisco.

World, the furthest boundary of the proverbial final frontier. This mythical location, of course, only adds to the city's romance and legend. From its origins as a Gold Rush outpost, San Francisco has captured the imaginations of the world's pioneers and frontiersman. Generation after generation, San Francisco has attracted those who wish to make that metaphorical journey Westward in search of new frontiers.

San Francisco has been home to some of history's most colorful personalities and frontiersmen. The early gold surveyors, pioneers and sailors gave way to waves of merchants, barons and boomtown entrepreneurs, immigrants, poets, writers, artists, bankers, prostitutes, bums and rapscallions - all before the turn of the century.

In modern times, San Francisco has stood at the edge of cultural frontiers and has often been called the New Bohemia. Progressive idealism has been San Francisco's trademark. In the 1950s, the Beat Generation thrived in

Two typical aspects of San Francisco, the Transamerica Pyramid seen from Chinatown, and the Financial District.

4

San Francisco, transforming North Beach's cafes, wine bars and jazz clubs into the breeding ground of a revolutionary new form of artistic self-expression.

Less than a decade later, Flower Power descended on San Francisco, again transforming the city and symbolizing the ideals of an entire generation of Americans. In the 1970s and '80s, socio-political movements like free speech, gay rights, holistic health and the environment kept the city at the forefront of progressive thought and action.

What is amazing about San Francisco is its ability to reinvent itself over and over again. Less than 150 years ago, San Francisco was a backwater city of tents and mud. Today the city is home to a new breed of pioneer and frontiersman, the technological wizards of Silicon Valley who rule the cyber universe.

San Francisco is a major international city. After New York, it is the second most densely populated city in the U.S. Yet, San Francisco's inherent natural beauty and its powerful human character belie that fact. Unlike so many other modern metropolises - hollow canyons of glass, steel and brick - San Francisco has both heart and soul.

SECTION ONE

DOWNTOWN

Wells Fargo Bank History Museum ◆ 24

Jackson Square Historical District ◆ 26

Transamerica Pyramid ◆ 22

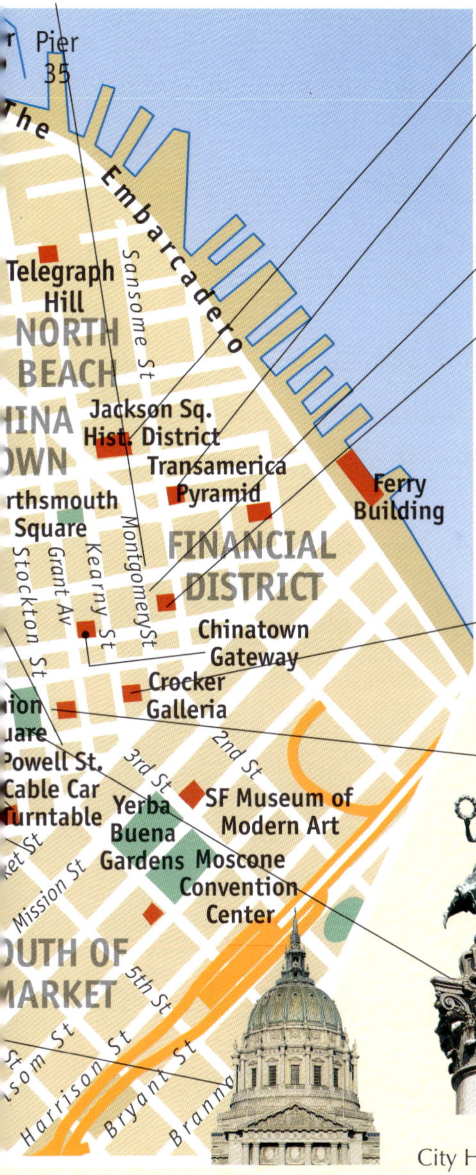

Merchant's Exchange Building ◆ 24

Pacific Coast Stock Exchange ◆ 28

Crocker Galleria ◆ 16

Maiden Lane ◆ 11

Union Square, the *Victory* ◆ 8

City Hall ◆ 31

7

UNION SQUARE

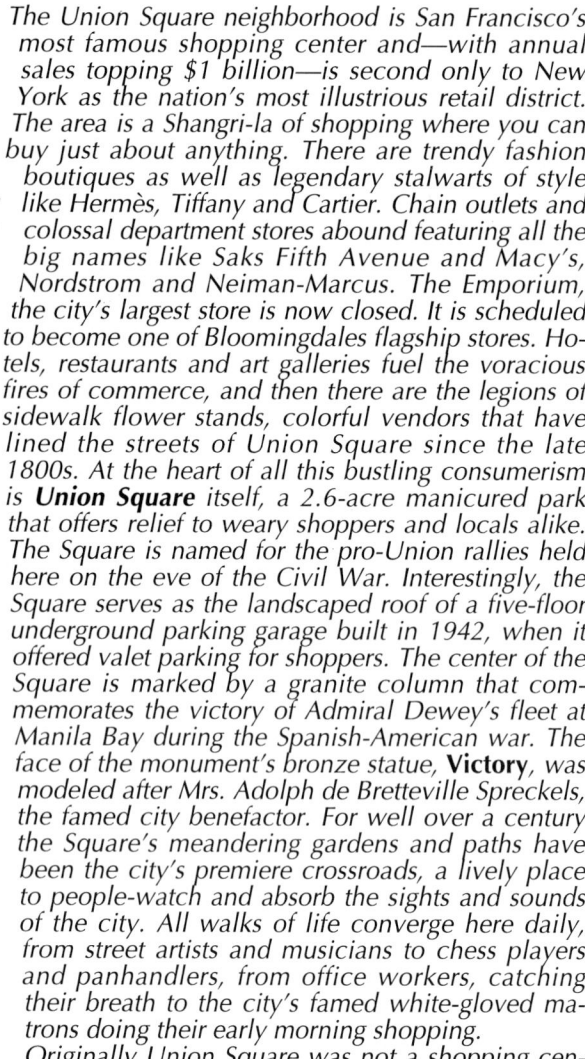

The Union Square neighborhood is San Francisco's most famous shopping center and—with annual sales topping $1 billion—is second only to New York as the nation's most illustrious retail district. The area is a Shangri-la of shopping where you can buy just about anything. There are trendy fashion boutiques as well as legendary stalwarts of style like Hermès, Tiffany and Cartier. Chain outlets and colossal department stores abound featuring all the big names like Saks Fifth Avenue and Macy's, Nordstrom and Neiman-Marcus. The Emporium, the city's largest store is now closed. It is scheduled to become one of Bloomingdales flagship stores. Hotels, restaurants and art galleries fuel the voracious fires of commerce, and then there are the legions of sidewalk flower stands, colorful vendors that have lined the streets of Union Square since the late 1800s. At the heart of all this bustling consumerism is **Union Square** itself, a 2.6-acre manicured park that offers relief to weary shoppers and locals alike. The Square is named for the pro-Union rallies held here on the eve of the Civil War. Interestingly, the Square serves as the landscaped roof of a five-floor underground parking garage built in 1942, when it offered valet parking for shoppers. The center of the Square is marked by a granite column that commemorates the victory of Admiral Dewey's fleet at Manila Bay during the Spanish-American war. The face of the monument's bronze statue, **Victory**, was modeled after Mrs. Adolph de Bretteville Spreckels, the famed city benefactor. For well over a century the Square's meandering gardens and paths have been the city's premiere crossroads, a lively place to people-watch and absorb the sights and sounds of the city. All walks of life converge here daily, from street artists and musicians to chess players and panhandlers, from office workers, catching their breath to the city's famed white-gloved matrons doing their early morning shopping.

Originally Union Square was not a shopping center at all. Quite the contrary, it was a focus of religious life, primarily for Jews and Protestants. After Jasper O'Farrell cleared the Square as a public space in 1847, no fewer than three Protestant churches lined the Square, and a fourth was less than a block away along with a Jewish temple. By the close of the nineteenth century, all but one of

The bronze statue Victory stands high above Union Square.

these places of worship had moved out of the neighborhood.

In the latter part of the nineteenth century, Union Square was also recognized as the home and playground of the city's rich and mighty. Several private clubs sprung up along Post Street to cater to the city's social elite, many of whom lived conveniently nearby.

Lined with Victorian mansions and townhouses, Sutter Street was the most fashionable and prestigious place of residence at that time. As the area became more crowded, however, the aristocracy moved west to even grander domains in Pacific Heights. Businesses swooped in to convert these palatial private houses into shops and stores, and thus one of the nation's retail capitals was born.

Today Union Square is marked by several notable structures. To the west stands the **Westin St. Francis Hotel**, as visually commanding today as it was when it was constructed in 1904 by Charles T. Crocker. Designed by Bliss & Faville, this skyscraper hotel drastically altered the complexion of the neighborhood and boldly heralded the arrival of commerce to Union Square. Although the hotel suffered severe earthquake damage in 1906, its steel-frame construction saved the

Union Square is San Francisco's most famous shopping center.

building from annihilation. When it was rebuilt in 1908, the St. Francis had 750 rooms, more than any other hotel on the Pacific coast. The hotel was expanded again in later years, so the building now has 1,200 rooms and spans the entire park block. In addition, there are seven restaurants on the premises, and the Grand Ballroom holds more than 1,500 people. In 1972 William Pereira Associates added a tower and exterior elevators that offer an impressive view of the city.

The department stores on the Square are revered more for fashionable merchandise than innovative architecture, but for the most part the buildings do accommodate their setting—a statement that cannot be made for most retail monoliths. Designed by Hellmuth, Obata & Kassabaum in 1981, **Saks Fifth Avenue** commands the northwest corner of Union Square. While not as bold visually as the New York City flagship, the building's round corners and subtle colors distinguish the exterior. Inside the architecture is less successful, as the jumble of escalators diminishes all sense of space.

Built by Philip Johnson and John Burgee in 1982 on the southeast corner of Union Square, **Neiman-Marcus** rose at the expense of an old favorite, the City of Paris general store, which had occupied the spot since 1896. The superb four-story rotunda of City of Paris, designed by Bakewell and Brown in 1908, is in fact housed within the

The atrium of Neiman-Marcus on Stockton Street.

*dramatic red granite and glass façade of Neiman-Marcus. The rotunda has beautiful belle époque plaster flourishes; the subtle, white and gold stained-glass canopy depicts a ship at sea—the symbol of Paris, France. In all, the preservation of the old store is perhaps the finest attribute of the new. Across the street along the south side of Union Square is **Macy's** department store, which spans an entire city block where I. Magnin once stood.*

Maiden Lane — On the east side of Union Square is the entrance to Maiden Lane, formerly and infamously known as Morton Street. Until the earthquake and fire of 1906 cleaned out the cribs with Biblical vengeance, Morton Street was lined with prostitutes and bordellos. The whole street was a red-light district with prostitutes flaunting their wares and soliciting passersby from open windows. Astoundingly, this few block stretch averaged almost two murders a week. Eventually the area's budding commerce transformed this street as well, and local entrepreneurs managed to change the street's name to convey the new ethic. Today Maiden Lane is a lovely pedestrian walkway lined with chic boutiques and fancy restaurants with outdoor dining in nice weather. It certainly has come a long way.

At 140 Maiden Lane is the outstanding **Circle Gallery** designed by Frank Lloyd Wright in 1949. Formerly a crystal and china shop known as V.C. Morris—the name is still visible in Wright's handsomely chiseled lettering—this building is one of the city's greatest architectural achievements. As in all of Wright's works, form and function are closely allied in the structure's architectural conceits: the circular design motifs used throughout the building gave a wink to the shapes of the plates and saucers displayed within. Circles appear subtly in every detail of the building, from the grand scheme of the architecture to the minute considerations of the furnishings.

Though the original building dates from 1911, Wright's renovation did not leave much trace of the former structure. Outside, Wright emphasized the play of light on the brickwork and the ornately detailed archway at the opening. Lights were placed along the façade's ornate molding, and the sidewalk at the entrance—now cemented over—even featured a semi-circle of lights under glass. Wright fans should appreciate the red square tile in the lower left corner of the façade that bears the architect's signature.

Inside, the spiral ramp leading to the upper floor was one of the precursors to Wright's design of the Guggenheim Museum in New York City. It rises gently to the skylighted ceiling, again emphasizing the nuance of light and space. Although the gallery displays contemporary art, don't forget to notice what's left of Wright's original walnut furniture, recognizable—of course—for its circle motif.

Above, the Powell Street Cable Car turntable at Hallidie Plaza is a great tourist attraction. Right, cable cars offer exquisite views of the city and bay.

Powell Street Cable-Car Turnaround — One of the hubs of the city's historic cable-car lines is the Powell Street turntable at Hallidie Plaza, where a lengthy line of tourists is always waiting to hop aboard. The wait can be a long one, but usually there is an array of street performers there to entertain. When the cable cars arrive at the turntable, the pit-stop is quite entertaining in itself. The cars come in, unload, get turned around manually by the cable car conductors and then dutifully load up for the next voyage. The whole process is charmingly awkward.

The first cable-car voyage was launched in 1873, when Scottish inventor Andrew Hallidie guided his car along Clay Street, navigating five treacherously hilly blocks en route to Chinatown. Hallidie, who had previously been a mine-cable engineer during California's Gold Rush, decided to implement the cable-car system after having witnessed a brutal accident involving a horse-drawn carriage on one of the city's notorious hills.

Quickly after their inaugural run, cable cars transformed the city. They represented a safe and efficient means of transportation. Neighborhoods that were previously deemed unsuitable for living suddenly became quite hospitable with the new trolley system. The network peaked just before the 1906 earth-

A suggestive image of a cable car with the Bay Bridge in the distance.

quake, when there were almost 600 cars and 110 miles of track. The earthquake and the ensuing fire did extensive damage, however. Many lines were not rebuilt, and others were replaced with electric trolleys. With the invention and proliferation of the automobile, the trolley system dwindled dramatically over the next fifty years. In an effort to stem the rapid deterioration of the lines, the city voted to preserve the trolley system in 1955. Nine years later, San Francisco's cable cars became the first moving National Historic Landmarks in the country. In 1986, a massive two-year, $60 million renovation was completed that again rejuvenated the trolleys. The entire system was overhauled. The cars' new seats and wheels and shiny coat of maroon, blue and gold paint were only the most obvious renovations. The tracks and cable vaults were replaced with deeper grooved rails and more flexible curves, and the pulleys and depression beams that guide each cable were restored. Many of the cable-car routes were redirected to flow with automobile traffic. The renovation task was enormous, but today the system shines in all its historic glory.

There are forty-four cars in the fleet today, with as many as twenty-seven climbing the hills at any given time. The city's seventeen miles of track are divided into three separate lines, of which the Powell-Hyde Line is said to offer the most panoramic views of the city as well as the most exciting curves. The faint of heart and stomach shouldn't worry about the curves, however, because each six-ton car travels at a steady, non-threatening 9.5 miles an hour. Each car is pulled along by a cable beneath the street that moves by the turning of an enormous, fourteen-foot wheel housed in a car barn. If you want to see how all this works, the historic **Cable Car Barn** at Washington and Mason streets was completely renovated and restored to its original appearance in the 1986 refurbishment. Each wheel and cable is constantly in motion, so the cable-car operator starts and stops the car by mechanically gripping and releasing the cable. The system seems almost too simple for our hurly-burly world, but thirteen million passengers climb on the cable cars each year—that's almost 36,000 a day!

THEATRES

The Theater District — The six or seven blocks west of Union Square comprise what is commonly known as San Francisco's Theater District. San Franciscans have been ardent theater supporters since the days of the Gold Rush, when miners were known to shower stage starlets with bags of gold dust. Though in many ways cut off from the cultural milieu of the other world capitals, San Franciscans were remarkably sophisticated even in the early years. With great fanfare, the city's first opera house opened in 1851. **Lotta's Fountain**, located at the intersection of Geary, Kearny and Market streets, stands to this day as a testament of the city's lasting appreciation of the performing arts. The fountain commemorates the career of actress Lotta Crabtree, who began her career in San Francisco as a dancer during the Gold Rush.

During the 1920s, vaudeville acts set up shop in the Union Square area and constructed lavish theaters in the process. In fact the best of these theaters remain today, with their ornate fixtures and elaborately carved fittings well preserved. Several of these theaters can rival any house on New York City's Broadway in terms of visual opulence as well as outstanding production. The **Curran**, **Golden Gate** and **Orpheum Theaters** all seat up to 2,000 people and receive top-notch musicals directly from the stages of New York and London. The **American Conservatory Theater (ACT)**, one of the most highly respected repertory companies in the country, has recently returned to the 1,300-seat **Geary Theater**, which underwent major refurbishment after the 1989 Loma Prieta earthquake. For six years after the quake, ACT held performances at two other medium-sized theaters in the area, **Theater on the Square** and **Stage Door Theater**, both renowned for more experimental productions. The avant-garde is also well represented at the nearby **Marines Memorial Theater** and the **New Conservatory Theater Center**.

SHOPPING

San Francisco Shopping Centre — Another shopping attraction in the Union Square neighborhood is the San Francisco Shopping Centre, a ten-level vertical shopping mall with over one hundred shops, cafés and restaurants. The Centre looks quite impressive—even along this block of stately neoclassical buildings. The façade is appropriately cast in gray granite, and the roofline is recessed to give the building a loftier aspect and to allow more sunlight into Hallidie Plaza across the street. The atrium at the pinnacle is covered with a large steel and glass dome that opens when the weather is good.

A vertiginous view of the Nordstrom department store, located in the S.F. Shopping Centre.

Inside, the building is equally impressive. The top four levels of the Centre were converted into a spectacular **Nordstrom** department store in 1988 by architecture firm Whisler-Patri. Besides sumptuous merchandise, one of the main attractions here is the country's first semi-spiral escalators. Designed by Mitsubishi, these three pairs of curved escalators wind along the building's central well up to the domed roof.

The Centre also boasts another interesting feature that is discreetly hidden from public view: two sixty-foot-long elevators lift thirty-ton trucks from street level to the building's top floors, making deliveries a cinch.

Crocker Galleria — When Crocker Bank built its towering pink granite headquarters in 1982, it included a glass-roofed, barrel-vaulted shopping arcade, the Crocker Galleria. The thirty-eight story tower, designed by Skidmore, Owings & Merrill, has since been renamed Telesis Tower, but the Galleria remains.

The three-level Galleria is modeled after the enormous Galleria Vittorio Emanuele in Milan, Italy. Although much smaller, the Crocker has an expansive central plaza under the vaulted skylight roof and over fifty stores and restau-

On this page, two images of the Crocker Galleria's glass promenade.

rants. Fashion boutiques include such fabulously chic as Gianni Versace and Ralph Lauren.
Across Sutter Street is the impressive **Hallidie Building**, designed by Willis Polk in 1917 and believed to feature the world's first glass curtain wall façade, which is projected a few feet beyond the reinforced concrete structure. For that alone, the Hallidie is San Francisco's most important building, setting an historic precedent in the annals of modern urban architecture. Built for the University of California, the building was named after Andrew Hallidie, inventor of the cable car and a university regent. The façade is further enhanced by beautiful, Regency-inspired fire escapes and an imposing Venetian Gothic cornice.

FINANCIAL DISTRICT

San Francisco's Financial District is as powerful commercially as it is elegant visually. One of the four largest business centers in the United States, the Financial District rises dramatically on the horizon as one approaches the city, as some 225,000 commuters do every day to get to work. The natural terrain of the city gives the downtown area an ethereal aspect, that of the proverbial city on the hill, a financial mecca indeed. Despite its commercial power, the Financial District is actually quite compact, designed on a very human scale. All points of commerce are within easy walking distance.
"Wall Street West" is home to some of the largest corporations in the world, including Chevron, Transamerica, Bechtel, Pacific Gas & Electric, Bank of America and Levi Strauss, an international favorite. Despite the presence of these financial giants, the vast majority of businesses are small, with fewer than ten employees. Not surprisingly,

Aerial view of Financial District.

the proximity of Silicon Valley has made the Financial District one of the world leaders in technology and communications development.

The landscape of the Financial District was drastically altered by the Gold Rush of 1849 and the rise of the "instant city," which transformed San Francisco from a quiet port of less than one thousand people to a major metropolis of over twenty thousand. Amazingly, much of the District was once covered by the San Francisco Bay. Montgomery Street was the eastern frontier of the city, poised on what was known as Yerba Buena Cove.

Inadvertently and over many years, the city expanded eastward: an ocean wall was built in the Bay to facilitate the unloading of cargo ships during the Gold Rush, while at the same time Yerba Buena Cove was slowly being graded by overuse. The arrival of thousands of ships depleted the shores of the Cove; where necessary, mud flats were filled in with sand and dirt taken from nearby hills. Over the course of a few decades, the Cove was entirely covered with landfill and eventually joined the sea wall. Many of the buildings we see on the eastern shore today, therefore, were built on land claimed from the sea.

Within a few years of the Gold Rush and before the Cove could be filled in, however, Montgomery Street was the focus of the city's finances. Because they were equipped to weigh and buy the gold dust being unloaded at port, waterfront shop keepers became bankers almost overnight. Soon Montgomery Street was lined with banks, and the surrounding area attracted luxury retail merchants. In 1854 the Gold Rush went bust in a fit of rash speculation. The Panic of Black Friday ensued, forcing many banks to close. Nevertheless, the Financial District was born.

In the 1890s the Victorian city was transformed by the iron- and steel-frame, brick-clad skyscrapers that arose in the Financial District. The **Chronicle Building** at Market and Kearny streets became San Francisco's first skyscraper in 1889. This home of the San Francisco Chronicle was designed by the Chicago firm of Burnham and Root. Although the building still stands, unfortunately the façade lost most of its charm when it was "modernized" in 1962. Thankfully, a few blocks away on Montgomery Street, Burnham and Root's **Mills Building** appears today much as it did upon construction in 1891. Its Romanesque Revival façade retains the nascent glory of the California skyscraper.

The proliferation of skyscrapers at the turn of the century greatly expanded downtown San Francisco and drastically altered the look of the whole city. When the earthquake

Three aerial views of the Financial District. The famed Transamerica Pyramid stands out among the city skyscrapers and against the panorama of the bay.

Several buildings in the Financial District are renowned for their fine, intricate masonry. The Royal Insurance Building and the Pacific Gas and Electric Company. are among the well-chiseled.

struck in 1906, there were over twenty steel-frame skyscrapers in the Financial District alone. Although fires gutted the insides of many skyscrapers, the steel frames resisted fire damage and made rebuilding possible. When the city was reconstructed in the following years, the pre-fire skyscrapers remained as models. The rebuilt city, therefore, had a remarkable architectural coherence. In the mid-1920s another building boom swept through the Financial District, again changing the skyline. The new wave of skyscrapers were taller and—with towers receding from the street—appeared to soar, indeed. The **Shell Building** on Bush Street and the Miller and Pleuger-designed **450 Sutter Street** are the best examples of this architectural era, which ended soundly with the Stock Market Crash of 1929. Not until the 1960s would the downtown area undergo any major architectural projects, and then it was only to produce sterile plazas and cold office towers, a tradition that would continue for years to come.

Buildings and skyscrapers in the Financial District.

Transamerica Pyramid — The Transamerica Pyramid has become San Francisco's signature landmark. In both size and majesty, nothing dominates the city's skyline quite like the Pyramid. At 853 feet, the Pyramid is the city's most towering skyscraper—only the Sutro Television Tower atop Twin Peaks is a taller structure. The Pyramid is visible at points throughout the city and, indeed, from across the Bay as well. Although the building is for the most part universally embraced today, it has not enjoyed such acclaim for long. In fact, when the building was completed in 1972 after almost three years of construction, it caused great controversy for being too big, too corporate, too flashy for quiet San Francisco.

Designed by Los Angeles architect William Pereira and Associates, the Pyramid climbs forty-eight stories. Originally, Transamerica chairman John Beckett had wanted the building to soar to one thousand feet and fifty-five stories. The plan was downsized after broad civic protests. As it is, the building's curtain walls are made up of three-thousand quartz-aggregate concrete panels that weigh three-and-a-half tons each. The concrete-and-steel foundation, sunk more than fifty feet into the ground, weighs more than 30,000 tons. The structure is

The iconic Transamerica Pyramid.

topped by a hollow, illuminated, 212-foot spire. All together, the project cost almost $45 million. Today the Pyramid is home to more than fifty firms, which in turn employ more than 1,500 people.

Tourists and city residents alike enjoy the changing art exhibits in the lobby, and the observation area on the 27th floor provides excellent northern views of such landmarks as Coit Tower, Alcatraz and the Golden Gate Bridge. Directly to the east is **Transamerica Redwood Park**, a half-acre landscaped park designed by Tom Galli. This miniature forest includes eighty redwood trees transplanted from the Santa Cruz Mountains. The Pyramid is the eponymously-named home office of Transamerica,

San Francisco is a city of contrasts. Here the Transamerica Pyramid confronts a lovely Victorian.

which was founded by A.P. Giannini in 1928 as a bank holding company. Today the business is an enormous corporate conglomerate with 11,000 employees worldwide and assets estimated at more than $32 billion.

The building site, located at the end of Columbus Avenue on the fringe of North Beach's cafe culture, was bought by Transamerica for $8 million in 1969. The location itself has an interesting history, having once been the site of the city's prime literary and artistic crossroads. The Montgomery Block building, affectionately known as the Monkey Block, was built in 1853 and stood here for over a century. For decades the building was the largest west of the Mississippi, and perhaps the most important meeting place in the West as well. Though intended as offices for prominent businesses, the building was eventually taken over by writers and newspapermen. At one point the building was more of a live-in dormitory for bohemian poets, artists and political radicals. Mark Twain met a fireman named Tom Sawyer here in the basement steam baths. George Sterling, Maynard Dixon, Ambrose Pierce, Bret Harte and Joaquin Miller were among those who frequently pulled up a stool at the bar. Sun Yat-sen, who would later overthrow China's Manchu Dynasty, published *Young China* from his second-floor office here.

Merchant's Exchange Building — As one of the original steel-frame buildings in San Francisco and as a survivor of the 1906 earthquake, the Merchant's Exchange is one of the city's most important office buildings. Designed by Willis Polk of the Chicago architecture firm D.H. Burnham in 1903, the Exchange was one the prototypes for the post-quake building boom of the early twentieth century. Today the Exchange also happens to house some of the city's finest public art. The building's classical façade is given a focus by the stately twin columns around the entrance. Inside, the marble lobby features ornately designed elevator doors and wonderful model ships. The skylight above creates a Pantheon-esque effect. The lobby leads to the entrance of the **Grain Exchange Hall**, once the commercial center of the entire West Coast, and today the office of First Interstate Bank. In days of yore, when shipping was the city's primary commerce, a look-out posted on the roof of the Exchange would herald the arrival of ships to the traders and businessmen gathered in the great hall below. Although primitive in means, the bustling atmosphere was not unlike the floor of our modern-day stock exchanges. Constructed like the portico of an ancient Greek temple, the Grain Exchange opens onto a hall hung with a series of large oil paintings by marine painters William Coulter and Nils Hagerup. Coulter is renowned for his detailed depictions of turn-of-the-century ports and sailing vessels. The collection here, painted around 1910, focuses on San Francisco's shipping industry and is considered among his best work. Paintings like *Arrived, All Well* and *War Time* give wonderful perspectives of this newly-born capital of the West.

Wells Fargo Bank History Museum — Inspired by Gold Rush fever, upstate New Yorkers Henry Wells and William George Fargo met with their associates in New York City to create a joint stock company in March

Wells Fargo Bank History Museum: A Gold Rush Balance Scales and, preceding page, a well-rigged Stagecoach.

of 1852. The company was to act as a commercial liaison between New York City and San Francisco, conducting banking and other business ventures between the two coastal cities and all points in between. In July of 1852, Wells, Fargo & Company opened shop on San Francisco's Montgomery Street, not ten feet from where the Wells Fargo Bank History Museum stands today. Only three years later, Wells Fargo was a financial powerhouse, with fifty-five offices nationwide; by 1890, there were 2,600 Wells Fargo branches across the country. The Museum, then, is well-deserved and provides a fascinating historical perspective of the meteoric rise of a fledgling business venture and—at the same time—San Francisco itself. The Museum is connected to the bank's central office, located around the corner on California Street. The 4,400-square-foot Museum exhibits artifacts from the Gold Rush and the dawn of transcontinental travel: mining equipment, gold nuggets, period photographs and early banking paraphernalia are on display. The crowd favorite is the authentic nineteenth-century, red-and-yellow-painted stagecoach made in Concord, New Hampshire. Upstairs, visitors can sit in a reproduction stagecoach while listening to a narration describing the travails of the interminable voyage from the East. Also upstairs is a display commemorating Charles E. Bolton, alias Black Bart, who robbed twenty-eight stagecoaches in the 1870s and 80s. Besides mastering the art of highway robbery, Black Bart was famous for the notes of poetry he left at the scene of his crimes. Amazingly, Black Bart was apprehended after carelessly dropping a handkerchief that was traced to a laundry on Bush Street. Black Bart served only four years at San Quentin State Penitentiary, after which he was paroled for good behavior. He was never heard from again.

Jackson Square Historical District — Designated the city's first historic district, Jackson Square was the only downtown area left standing after the 1906 earthquake.

Most of these brick buildings date back to the 1850s and give an idea of what the city looked like during the Gold Rush and the early days of the "instant city." What remains of the district, bounded by Montgomery and Sansome streets and Jackson and Washington streets, constitutes what was the city's original financial district, which then became the city's most nefarious prostitution quarters.

In San Francisco's earliest days, both commerce and retail were centered in Portsmouth Square and what is now the Jackson Square Historical District. Montgomery Street bordered the Bay at Yerba Buena Cove, and there the city had decided to set up shop. The Gold Rush and the subsequent influx of thousands of miners and traders to the city changed all that. The city grew twenty-fold almost overnight, and what had been the focus of the city's financial life suddenly got a new address. The physical transformation of the city, the expansion of the eastern frontier into Yerba Buena Cove, changed where the city did business. Commercial interests moved to where the money was. The Gold Rush trade was happening along the expanding shipping ports to the south and east. The city's present-day Financial District was born then and there, leaving Jackson Square to another fate.

Bottom and opposite, historical buildings in the Jackson Square area.

As businesses began to move out of the Jackson Square area, a new element began to move in. Gold Rush fever brought thousands of men westward seeking fame and fortune. Most of them didn't have much luck finding either, and all of them were lonely and desperate for companionship. They tended to drift to San Francisco for comfort, and the city was all too eager to please. The area around Jackson Square, in fact, became known as the Barbary Coast—named after an infamous port in Northern Africa—because of its boundless perversion and wickedness. Drinking, gambling and prostitution became big business.

Pacific Street was the Barbary Coast's main thoroughfare and became known as "Terrific Pacific." A line of bordellos, raunchy saloons and gambling halls stretched six blocks from the waterfront. Certain stretches earned titles like "Murderer's Corner", "Battle Row", and "Dead Man's Alley". In 1908 The Dash opened at Pacific and Kearny and became the city's first gay bar. Lawlessness reigned and violence and debauchery were its henchmen. Casual death was almost as commonplace as casual sex. The lure of the Barbary Coast was so great that ship captains had to "Shanghai" prospective sailors in waterfront bars. The practice involved knocking out bar cus-

27

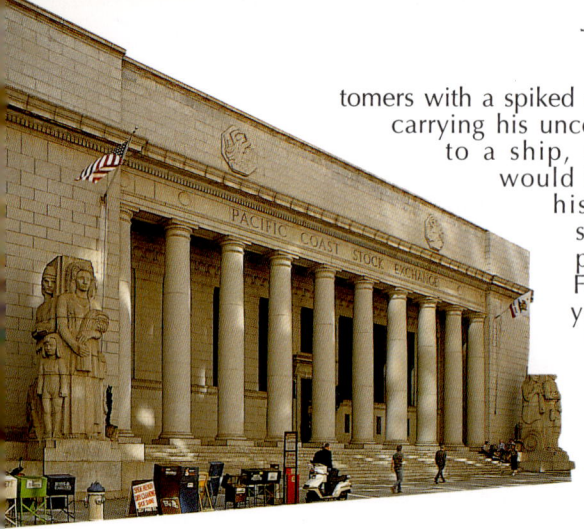

tomers with a spiked drink and then carrying his unconscious body to a ship, on which he would have to work his passage to some distant port.

For almost sixty years the Barbary Coast partied on, to the moral outrage of many of the city's governors. In April of 1906 the earthquake and fire destroyed much of the Coast, although amazingly Jackson Square itself was spared. Mired in six square miles of smoking embers, the Square stood unscathed, the only downtown survivor. So the debauchery continued, and only in 1917 did civic decree put a damper on the festivities. Even so, the newly-coined International Settlement endured, in more modest terms, until the 1950s.

Today, the elegant, tree-lined streets of the Barbary Coast are thoroughly gentrified. The area is now known as Jackson Square, although no square is to be found. Designers, architects and antique dealers occupy many of these historic brick houses and cast-iron office buildings. The east side of the **700 block of Montgomery Street** has several of these notable buildings, as does the **400 block of Jackson Street** around the corner. **Gold Street** has the most well-preserved stretch of 1850's architecture; the **Bank of Lucas, Tuner & Company** at the western end was constructed in 1853 and managed by William Tecumseh Sherman, who would later burn Atlanta as a Union general in the Civil War.

Pacific Coast Stock Exchange — Outside of New York, the Pacific Coast Stock Exchange is the country's largest stock market. Financially, the Exchange is the heart and soul of the district's bustling commerce: through the open front door, visitors can see the frantic trading on the floor. Architecturally, however, the building presents a somewhat awkward mix of classical and Moderne styles.

Originally designed by Cleveland architect J. Milton Dyer in 1915 to house the U.S. Subtreasury, the Exchange building has a complex history. After the Stock market Crash of 1929, the government moved out and the San Francisco Stock Exchange moved in. Dyer's classical façade, that of a somber granite temple adorned with a

Doric colonnade, was recommissioned by Miller and Pfleuger in 1930 to give the building a more contemporary look. The overhaul included adding Moderne bas-relief motifs to the building's cornice and massive sculptures, designed by Ralph Stackpole, along the entryway. To the right is Stackpole's *Man and His Inventions*, to the left *Mother Earth*.

Miller and Pfleuger were also commissioned to design the twelve-story granite office tower behind the Exchange. Again Stackpole was called upon to create a monumental high-relief carving, *The Progress of Man,* over the entrance. The lobby is equally muscular, bedecked with black marble and a geometric, gold-leaf ceiling. Upstairs is the City Club, a private watering hole reserved for members of the stock exchange. Along the way in the club's two-story stairwell is Diego Rivera's superb mural *Allegory of California*, which depicts California as bounteous, life-bearing Mother.

On these pages, the Pacific Coast Stock Exchange, the largest stock market in the U.S. outside of New York.

CIVIC CENTER

San Francisco's Civic Center is renowned as the finest collection of Beaux Arts buildings in the United States. One man can be credited with much of the Civic Center's brilliance: Daniel Burnham, the Chicago architect commissioned in 1904 to design the city's master plan. Burnham, along with his young assistant, Willis Polk, were called upon by former Mayor James Phelan and several other prominent city benefactors to remedy the city's blight of unattractive architecture. Although political scandal and the catastrophe of 1906 delayed construction of the Civic Center until after Burnham's death, the city wisely followed his recommendations and created a wonderful public space. Mayor "Sunny" Jim Rolph was the man who actually carried out the plans for the Civic Center. He was a stalwart supporter of City Beautiful principles, and under his guidance San Francisco achieved one of the world's finest civic centers.

Aerial view of San Francisco's Civic Center.

The imposing face of City Hall in the Civic Center.

City Hall — Designed in 1915 by prominent Bay Area architect Arthur Brown, City Hall is the centerpiece of the Civic Center and the grandest public space in the city. It is a monument imbued with civic pride—not only for its beauty, but also for the hope it fostered during a tumultuous era in the city's history. On April 18, 1906, an earthquake shook the city and leveled the old City Hall, which stood where the Main Public Library is today. An estimated 8.25 on the Richter scale—ten times more powerful than any other to hit the city before or since—the quake of 1906 killed 674 people and left 250,000 homeless. The catastrophe consumed 28,000 buildings, and property damages alone totaled $400 million.

The city was in shambles and desperate for leadership. For years city government had been thwarted by scandal and corruption. After the catastrophe, reform-minded voters and politicians alike united to clean up the ruined municipality—inside and out. Corrupt city bosses were brought to justice: Abe Ruef pleaded guilty to extortion and was sentenced to fourteen years in San Quentin; ex-Mayor Schmitz was found guilty of twenty-seven counts graft and bribery. Construction of the $8.8 million City Hall, therefore, symbolized the dawning of a new political era, one led for almost twenty years by Republican mayor and future governor James Rolph, Jr. So large were Rolph's contributions to the city, upon his death in 1934 he was buried under City Hall's majestic dome, the finest building constructed during the glorious City Beautiful era. Brown's design won the $25,000 competition for City Hall, beating out almost eighty other entries. His Ecole des Beaux-Arts training in Paris is evident in the building's French Renaissance style. Other former students of the Ecole des Beaux-Arts included Jean Louis Bourgeois, who designed the interiors, and Henri Crenier, who created the vast, ornate array of sculptures. The building's huge lead and copper dome was modeled after St. Peter's Basilica in Rome. The dome itself is over 301 feet tall, rising three feet higher than that of the nation's capital. While the building has a sober, gray granite façade ornamented with stately Doric columns, the interior is much more lavish. The ceiling of the rotunda is decorated with a cartouche depicting a ship at sea. Exuberant Corinthian columns accent pink Tennessee marble floors and ornate, Indiana sandstone walls. A radiant sunburst clock hangs on one wall under an impressive sculpture of Father Time. The iron and bronze light fixtures and railings were made by Leo J. Myberg and represent some of the best Beaux Arts metalwork in the city. The first landing of the grand, flowing Baroque staircase is the city's most important public stage. In more recent history, City Hall was the sight of the assassination of Mayor George Moscone and Supervisor Harvey Milk by disgruntled ex-supervisor Dan White on November 28, 1978. Supervisor Diane Feinstein was then named Mayor of the city, and her political career soared in the following years. In 1999, a major seismic upgrade and restoration of City Hall was completed under the guidance of Mayor Willie Brown.

War Memorial Opera House — Opera is one of the primary social and cultural events in San Francisco. From the gala season-

The stately façade of War Memorial Opera House.

opener in September through December, the War Memorial Opera House is the place to be. Designed by Arthur Brown and dedicated to the memory of World War I soldiers, the lavish opera house opened on October 15, 1932. It was the first municipally financed opera house in the country and has since become the centerpiece of the city's Performing Arts Center. The building seats 3,176, and productions here are astounding, renowned the world over. One of the nation's oldest and most revered dance companies, the San Francisco Ballet, performs here as well, beginning its season right after the opera closes. Some interesting bits of trivia: it was here in 1945 that the first United Nations charter was signed; six years later, the Opera House was again the focus of international affairs when it hosted the signing of the peace treaty between the U.S. and Japan, officially ending World War II.

Louise M. Davies Symphony Hall — Designed by architects Skidmore, Owings & Merrill in 1980, the Louise M. Davies Symphony Hall is home to the top-notch San Francisco Symphony. From September through May, the Symphony packs the 2,743-seat building. The hall was named after arts patron Louise M. Davies, who donated $5 million to the $33 million project. The building's wrap-around glass and granite façade, which has more than a faint resemblance to a futuristic space station, had few supporters upon its completion. To make matters worse, for years the hall's acoustics were considered only mediocre.

In 1992—after years of deliberation—the hall completed a $10 million acoustical and architectural renovation. To improve sound quality, a new audio system was installed. Furthermore, the interior

The sculpture gardens outside Louise M. Davies Symphony Hall.

walls of the hall were resculptured—using state-of-the-art computer technology—to reflect sound better. Occasionally, the Davies showcases what is the nation's largest concert hall organ. Built by the Ruffatti brothers of Padua, Italy, the organ consists of 9,235 computer-aided pipes.

New San Francisco Main Public Library — The New San Francisco Main Public Library replaced the old one next door on Larkin Street in 1996. The new building, designed principally by New York City architect James Freed in a Postmodern-Deconstructivist style, is more than two and a half times the size of its Beaux-Arts predecessor. Ironically, George Kelham's 1916 library had replaced a previous library destroyed in the 1906 quake; Kelham's granite-clad building was itself badly damaged in the 1989 Loma Prieta earthquake and closed for several months. The Asian Art Museum—currently in Golden Gate Park—is now preparing to move into the old library building. The new library represents the culmination of several building projects funded in the prosperous 1980s and built in the early 1990s. Incredibly, $30 million was raised privately to furnish the interior, making this project the largest public/private collaboration in the city's history. In a city of highly-educated, well-read citizens, it seems appropriate that this final project is a monumental library. The building is an interesting architectural amalgam. On one hand it seems to reflect the Civic Center's formal Beaux-Arts design, albeit with a Postmodern interpretation; on the other hand, it also appears to mimic the deconstructed, contemporary style of its neighbors on Grove and Hyde streets. Regardless, the building is quite striking and provocative to look at.

On these pages, examples of colorful Victorian houses you can find on Alamo Square.

A towering, five-story, glass-enclosed atrium dominates the building's interior. Like the old library, which was built around a monumental staircase, the new building also features a magnificent stairway that rises around the periphery of the atrium. The library houses more than a million books and is known for its collection of rare and handprinted editions—especially those printed in San Francisco. Within the library is the San Francisco History Room, the city's official archive. Both museum and research library, the History Room displays a rare collection of civic documents and photographs.

Alamo Square — Contrasting fabulously against both City Hall and the Financial District in the distance, Alamo Square is lined with so many lovely Victorian houses that the area has been declared an historic district. Included among these houses is the city's most famous row of colorful Victorians, "the painted ladies," which are set along the east side of this sloping square. Designed in an elaborate Queen Anne style, the "Six Sisters," as they are also known, were built by developer Matthew Kavanaugh in the mid-1890s. Today these ornate, gabled wooden houses are the most photographed private homes in San Francisco and appear on countless postcards.

Bill Graham Civic Auditorium — The oldest building in the Civic Center, the Bill Graham Civic Auditorium was designed in Beaux-Arts style by architect John Galen Howard. The building was completed just before City Hall during the architectural renaissance that followed the earthquake and fire of 1906. French pianist Camille Saint Saens was the featured performer at the building's 1915 inauguration. Since then, the 7,000 seat auditorium has become one of the city's most important performance sites.
In 1964 the building's name was changed in honor of Bill Graham, the famed rock music promoter who helped make San Francisco the epicenter of the country's 1960s cultural revolution. Graham opened such seminal '60s establishments as Winterland and the Fillmore East. In the process he brought such Rock & Roll legends as Jimi Hendrix and The Who to San Francisco. The cultural institution that is the Grateful Dead owes its existence in many ways to Bill Graham. He died in 1992, the most prolific promoter of all time.

Russian Hill, Lombard Street ◆ 52

Saints Peter and Paul ◆ 47

Chinatown, Tien Hau Temple ◆ 43

SF Art Institute ◆ 53

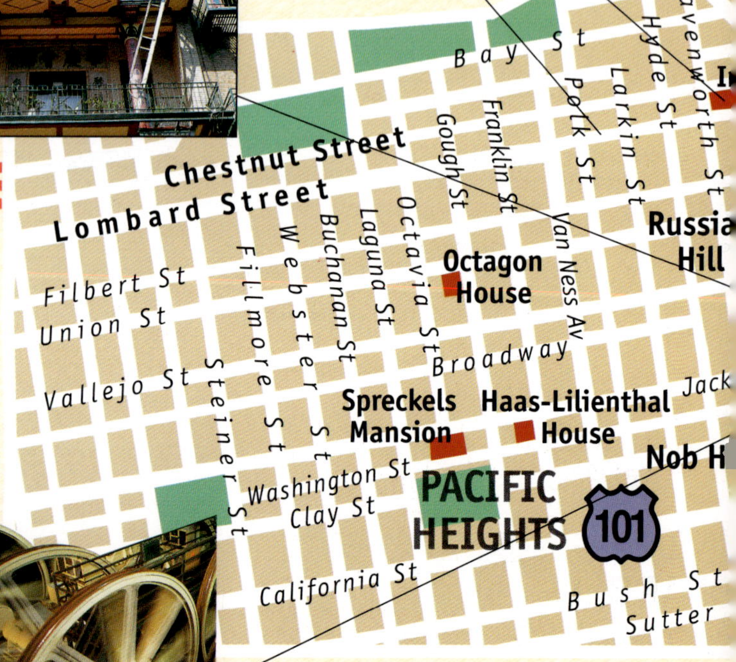

Cable Car Museum ◆ 59

36

SECTION TWO

CHINATOWN AND NORTH BEACH

Coit Tower
◆ 50

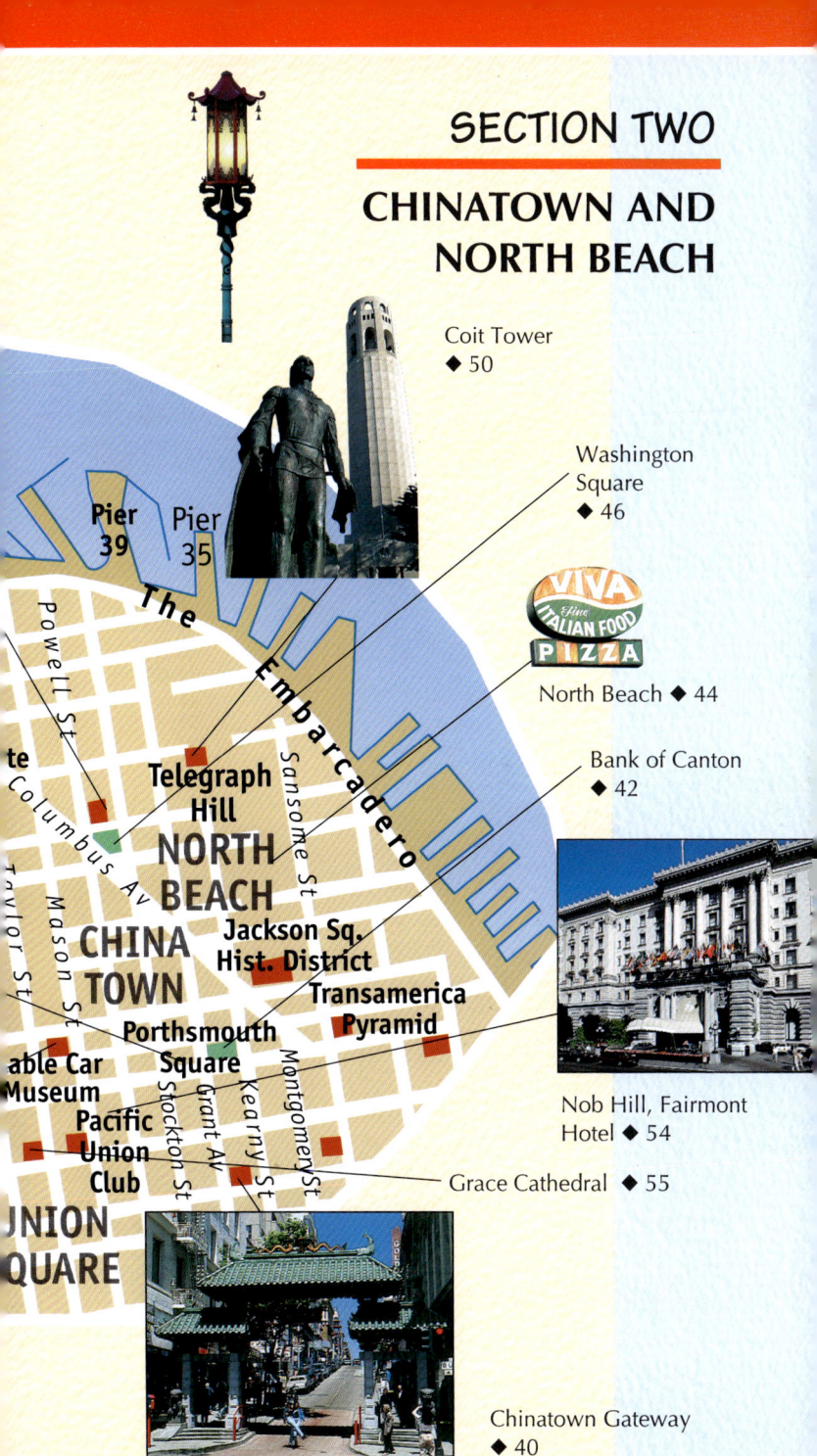

Washington Square
◆ 46

Pier 39 Pier 35

North Beach ◆ 44

Bank of Canton ◆ 42

Telegraph Hill

NORTH BEACH

Jackson Sq. Hist. District

CHINA TOWN

Transamerica Pyramid

Porthsmouth Square

Cable Car Museum

Pacific Union Club

Nob Hill, Fairmont Hotel ◆ 54

Grace Cathedral ◆ 55

UNION SQUARE

Chinatown Gateway
◆ 40

37

Chinatown: A familiar sight along Grant Avenue, a shopping street lined with dragon lamps.

CHINATOWN

The largest Chinese community on the West Coast, San Francisco's Chinatown is home to many of the Bay Area's 120,000 Chinese-Americans. In the U.S., only New York City's Chinatown is larger. Unlike New York's settlement, however, San Francisco's Chinatown is an integrated focus of city life.

The streets of Chinatown are noisy and garish and jam-packed with people. The atmosphere is quite hectic. One of the main draws here is cheap, delicious food: there are countless restaurants in Chinatown as well as numerous shops loaded with fresh fish and Chinese vegetables. On the weekends, it's a great place to go for dim sum, the traditional Chinese a la carte brunch, followed by a not-very-leisurely—but highly entertaining—stroll among the Chinese bric-a-brac shops, especially along **Grant Avenue**. Lined with dragon lamp-posts and buildings with fancy, turned-up tile rooves, Grant is the major tourist attraction in Chinatown. The streets here are raucous all day and late into the night.

To really enjoy Chinatown, however, one must get off the beaten track and explore. Then you might discover the culinary pleasures of **Stockton Street**, where locals do their shopping. Here one finds some of the freshest vegetables, produce and fish in *the city. Around the corner on Ross Alley, the **Golden Gate Fortune Cookie Company** allows customers to taste samples of their prophetic cookies—a local invention— which of course are now eaten around the world.*

*Although only two blocks long, **Waverly Place** is perhaps Chinatown's most intriguing find. During the Tong Wars of the late nineteenth century, Waverly Place was one of the scariest areas in the city. The streets were lined with brothels until the disaster of 1906, after which several Chinese community associations and two important temples were built. Today Waverly is known as "the street of painted balconies," for obvious reasons.*

The Transamerica Pyramid seen from Grant Avenue.

A motorized cable car at Chinatown Gateway.

Chinatown Gateway — Designed by Clayton Lee in 1970, the ornate Chinatown Gateway—also known as "Dragon's Gate"— serves as Chinatown's main portal. This monumental structure heralds the entrance to Chinatown's most bustling street for tourism, Grant Avenue.
The roof of the three-arched gate is covered with green tiles and decorated with totemic animal motifs.
These glazed ceramic figures include two dragons and two carps romancing a large pearl.
Alongside the gate are two vigilant stone lions suckling their cubs through their claws.

Portsmouth Square — With so much to see and do in San Francisco, it is easy to forget that Portsmouth Square was the birthplace of the city, once part of Mexican territory. In 1839 the Mexican government called on Swiss engineer Jean Jacques Vioget to plot out the town of what was then known as Yerba Buena, a mere cluster of adobe huts along Grant Avenue and simple frame buildings along the shore. The area Vioget plotted, with its short, narrow blocks and tiny lots, is still preserved in Chinatown. Portsmouth Square was the town's main plaza.

The square got its present name in 1846, when war broke out between Mexico and the United States. The *U.S.S. Portsmouth* swiftly took over the port town. In 1848, the Mexican peace treaty officially ceded the entire Southwest to the United States.

One year later, on May 12, 1849, Samuel Brennan, editor of the *California Star*, stood in Portsmouth Square and announced the discovery of gold in the foothills of the Sierra Nevada. Thus the California Gold Rush began, and San Francisco would soon become a major metropolis.

Portsmouth Square remained the hub of the growing city for the next decade or so, but in the 1860s business interests would shift to the landfill along the Bay in the southeast. Slowly the plaza declined in civic importance, although even today the square remains a busy and densely packed thoroughfare, a playground of sorts for Chinatown residents to commune, play cards and, in the morning, practice *t'ai chi*.

Murals in Chinatown.

When Robert Louis Stevenson lived in San Francisco in the late 1870s, he would sit in the square and absorb the sights and sounds of the bustling city. The **Hispaniola Monument** stands in the northwest corner of the square commemorating him. The **Goddess of Democracy** also rests here, a monument to the 1989 Tiananmen Square protests in Beijing. In the Holiday Inn across the footbridge from the square, the **Chinese Culture Center** features exhibitions of Chinese-American artists and writers.

Signboards in Grant Avenue.

Chinese Historical Society of America Museum — The Chinese Historical Society of America Museum is the only museum in the world devoted exclusively to Chinese-American history. This small basement museum courageously presents the countless Chinese contributions to American culture, especially in San Francisco, where so many Chinese emigrated. A series of photo panels traces the migration of Chinese in America and explains how Chinese-American culture has evolved. Arts and crafts, documents, photographs and innovative tools like a shrimp-peeling machine paint a vivid picture of how Chinese culture adapted to and influenced life in America. Among the favorite displays are a ceremonial dragon costume and a nineteenth-century, lacquered wood Taoist altar from Napa. Another is the "tiger fork," a weapon wielded during the the city's infamous Tong Wars, which were fought between rival clans to control Chinatown's prostitution and gambling in the late nineteenth century.

Bank of Canton — The most authentically Chinese building in all of Chinatown, the Bank of Canton is a wonderful spectacle to behold. Built in 1909, the three-tiered tower was home to the Chinatown Telephone Exchange until the 1950s, when the Bank of Canton acquired it. The building is an impressive work of architectural chinoiserie that has been well preserved by the Bank. It appears much like a pagoda, with the three upward-curving, ceramic-tiled rooves accenting the red walls and intricate, geometric tracery windows.

Originally, the telephone operators were all male and had to be fluent in English as well as five different Chinese dialects. They worked on the main floor and had sleeping quarters on the second. Since there is no Chinese alphabet, the telephone directory was arranged by street. A copy of an early telephone book—handwritten—is on display at the Chinese Historical Society.

Tien Hau Temple — Set among the painted balconies of Waverly Place, Tien Hau Temple occupies the top floor of a yellow-brick building designed in 1911 by the ubiquitous O'Brien Brothers. Dedicated to Tien Hau, Queen of Heaven and protector of seafarers and visitors, the Temple was founded in 1852 and is the oldest Chinese place of worship in the country.

At the top of three steep, wooden flights of stairs, the Temple opens onto another world entirely. The ceiling is covered with hundreds of gold and red lanterns, and the air is heavy with the scent of incense and burnt paper offerings. Red electric bulbs and oil candles light this narrow space, which is furnished with antiques from other temples destroyed when the Chinese were driven from remote California towns in the 1880s. Gift oranges lie on the carved altar, behind which a wooden statue of Tien Hau watches rather ominously.

A view of Tien Hau Temple.

NORTH BEACH

The beach that stretched between Telegraph and Russian Hills disappeared under landfill long ago, but North Beach remains one of the most exciting areas in the city. In many ways North Beach represents a lifestyle. On one hand it is known as "Little Italy" and is the historic center of the Italian community. On the other hand, North Beach is the traditional home of young bohemians and other radical intellectuals, the social fringe made famous by the Beatnik (a term coined by Herb Caen) generation of the 1950s. Conveniently, these two mythic forces—the Mediterranean and the angst-ridden—blend quite amicably in North Beach's exuberant cafe-oriented atmosphere.

Although North Beach is still intimately known as Little Italy, in fact the Italians were not the first nor the last to arrive here. Chilean prostitutes came first, lured by the Gold Rush in the 1850s. Then came the Irish, and finally the Italians after the turn of the century. By 1940, Italians were the largest foreign-born population in the city. The Chinese, however, were soon to arrive to North Beach. While Broadway was once considered the boundary between North Beach and Chinatown, during the 1960s the Chinese began crossing the border and settling in Little Italy. Today the population is more than fifty percent Chinese. Nevertheless, the Italian culture is a resilient one, and the neighborhood has retained its ethnic flavor. The annual Columbus Day Parade in October is still the biggest celebration of the year, and Italians still stream to the North Beach playground to play bocce. Most importantly, Italian cuisine still reigns supreme. North Beach remains the home of some of the city's best Italian restaurants, bakeries and cafes.

Columbus Avenue cuts a wide diagonal swath through North Beach and is home to several San Francisco institutions. **City Lights Bookstore** is the city's most famous literary institution. Opened by Beatnik poet Lawrence Ferlinghetti, City Lights grabbed the spotlight in 1956 with the publication of Allen Ginsberg's controversial poem *Howl*, which was widely condemned as obscene and pornographic. Across Jack Kerouac Street is **Vesuvio Cafe**, serving bohemians the likes of Dylan Thomas since 1949. Across Columbus is **Tosca Cafe**, a great place to see and be seen while listening to the jukebox play opera's greatest hits. The four blocks of Columbus between Filbert and Broadway are the busiest in Little Italy and feature back-to-back restaurants and cafes and are quite a scene on weekends.

Although tattoos and body piercings are not for everyone, the **Tattoo Art Museum** on Columbus Avenue certainly makes a strong case. This working tattoo parlor is lined with photographs of extravagant body decorations that make even the prudent pause and ponder.

More of North Beach's cultural treasures are found along **Upper Grant Avenue**, just north of Broadway and the **Condor Club,** where the modern world's first topless stage show was performed by Carol Doda in 1964. These blocks of restaurants, bars and coffee shops are some of the city's oldest and favorite places to spend a relaxing afternoon. A watering hole since 1861, **The Saloon** is one of these beloved city landmarks. At the corner of Vallejo, another is **Caffè Trieste**, the oldest coffeehouse in San Francisco and a popular hangout for Beatnik artists and writers in the 1950s. A time-honored tradition, Trieste offers live opera on Saturday afternoons. Just north is the **Lost and Found Saloon**, now a blues club but formerly the Coffee Gallery, another legendary Beatnik haunt.

The City Lights Bookstore.

Opposite, top, Vesuvio became one of North Beach's most famous bars during the Beat era. Bottom, a view of a street in North Beach.

Built in 1912 as an Italian community hall, **Club Fugazi** has been home to Beach Blanket Babylon, the city's most famous musical cabaret, for over two decades. Steve Silver's zany show is now a cultural institution, popular with locals and tourists alike. Although the themes change annually, each production is a bonfire of vanities, parodying the schmaltz of pop culture as well as that of the old city itself. The cabaret features a high-energy cast wearing outlandish costumes—especially bizarre, gigantic hats.

Above, bright lights, big city along Broadway between Chinatown and North Beach. Below, Benjamin Franklin's statue stands in the center of Washington Square.

Washington Square — The centerpiece of North Beach, Washington Square also happens to be one of the finest urban parks in the United States. With its peripheral shield of trees and broad expanse of lawn, Washington Square fits in perfectly against its urban backdrop. Although the park is the lowest depression between Russian and Telegraph hills, the sense of open space is powerful and refreshing. The surrounding buildings are conveniently unimposing—low and light-colored—and seem only to enhance the park's bucolic setting. The Square, in fact, has a cozy, small town feeling, which couldn't be more appropriate for North Beach life.

Reserved as a park by Mayor Jasper O'Farrell in 1847, Washington Square's current landscape was designed in 1955. In the center of this simple park stands a statue of Benjamin Franklin, a gift of H.D. Cogswell in 1879. Cogswell happened to be an outspoken teetotaler, which was apparent in 1979 when the time-capsule under the monument was opened to reveal tomes of temperance tracts. (Incidentally, the time capsule was refilled with a bottle of wine, a pair of Levi's jeans and some verses by Beatnik poet Lawrence Ferlinghetti; it will be reopened in 2079.) The monument's water taps—now long dry—are inscribed in the spirit of prohibition: "Cal Seltzer," "Vichy" and "Congress."

On the Columbus Avenue side of the park is a sentimental bronze statue that honors the city's volunteer firemen. Donated by the eccentric Lillie Hitchcock Coit, who was rescued from a burning house as a child, the monument was erected in 1933. Fittingly enough, it depicts two firemen with a rescued child. The park is the meeting place for young and old, especially the Italian - and Chinese-American families that live in the neighborhood. There is a certain social order here: older men tend to sit on the benches along Union Street, while young people stretch out on the lawn and children frolic in the playground area. Just like in small towns everywhere.

Saints Peter and Paul Roman Catholic Church — A majestic crown to the north side of the park, Saints Peter and Paul Church was designed by Charles Fantoni. The Romanesque church, distinguished by its stately twin spires, took two decades to construct and was finally dedicated in 1924. Interestingly, as the Church was being built, famed Hollywood director Cecil B. DeMille filmed the construction to depict the building of the Temple of Jerusalem in his 1953 film *The Ten Commandments*.

Still known as the Italian Cathedral, Saints Peter and Paul is a symbol of the Italian community even today, when the original Italian core has long dispersed and area is predominantly Chinese. The Church has been so central to the Italian community, in fact, that it has also been known as "Fishermen's Church" because so many Italians in the community once earned their living by fishing. A mass celebrating the Blessing of the Fleet is still held every

Washington Square.

October, when a procession migrates from the Church to Fisherman's Wharf. A testament to the Church's importance within the Italian community, local baseball hero Joe Di Maggio was photographed here after his marriage to Marilyn Monroe in 1957.
The building was constructed with a steel frame covered with white concrete. The interior is quite complex, notable for its many columns and ornate, extravagant altar, which depicts a beatific city adorned with a horizon of marble spires and life-size angels. The Church is filled with statues, mosaics and beautiful stained-glass windows.

The Romanesque façade of Saints Peter and Paul Catholic Church.

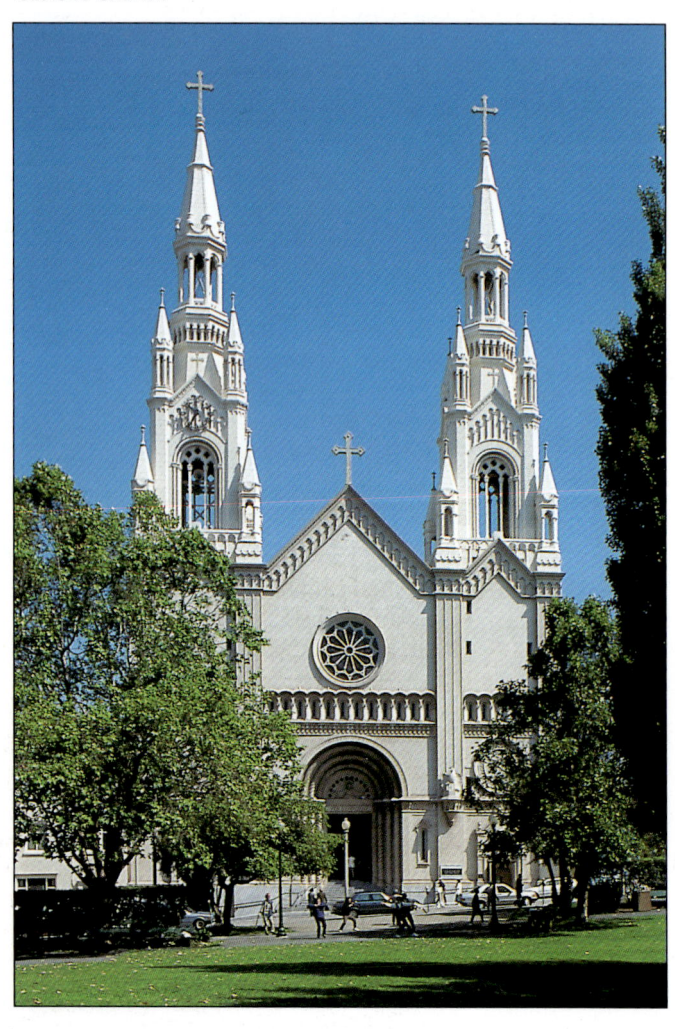

TELEGRAPH HILL

Telegraph Hill is another of San Francisco's quaint and prestigious residential districts. Although immigrants and bohemian types once roamed the streets, today only the city's affluent can afford to call the crest and eastern side of the "Hill" home. At 284 feet, the views over the Bay are nothing short of stunning. The hill received its name, in fact, after the Morse Code Signal Station was built on the hill's crest in 1853. The perch had a perfect view of the whole Bay, and the station, therefore, could quickly notify downtown business interests of incoming ships.

The hill was not always such a convenient place to live, hence the abundance of immigrants in the early years. All sides are incredibly steep, especially the vertiginous east side cliffs that were formed over years of quarrying. Up until 1914, the hillside was gradually carted away for landfill.

Although situated in the center of the city, the hill's treacherous terrain made it seem a remote outpost, an aspect that attracted bohemian types and artists. By the 1940s, however, the area had become gentrified and steep rents forced the artists to leave. The irony: artists made the hill chic, gave it cachet, which in turn attracted the monied classes, which drove up real estate prices.

At any rate, real estate prices have remained high, and Telegraph Hill remains one of the city's most affluent districts.

Two spectacular images of Coit Tower and Telegraph Hill.

View of Telegraph Hill. Bottom, the Christopher Columbus Statue, near Coit Tower.

Coit Tower — A memorial to San Francisco's volunteer firefighters, Coit Tower was constructed in 1933 at the summit of Telegraph Hill. Funds for the tower were provided by slightly daffy Lillie Hitchcock Coit, who left $100,000 towards beautifying the city upon her death in 1929. Lillie had demonstrated a lifelong obsession with fires and firefighters, so the tower seemed appropriate to commemorate both the city's eccentric benefactor as well as the platoons of San Francisco's Finest.

The 210-foot tower was designed by famed San Francisco architect Arthur Brown, who counts City Hall among his many other great projects. City lore suggests that the tower's fluted walls and porticoed observation deck were made to resemble the nozzle of a firehose. The architect, however, implored that was not his intention. Regardless, the reinforced concrete tower makes quite an impression—especially at night, when floodlights give the column an eerie, translucent quality. Sitting atop Telegraph Hill, Coit Tower has a commanding presence and can be seen from most of downtown as well as the North Bay. Likewise, in a city of many grand vistas, the view from Coit Tower's observation platform is unsurpassed.

The tower's lobby, however, is even more splendid than the views from the observation deck. The ground-floor hall is decorated floor-to-ceiling with a collection of gigantic murals that date back to the Great Depression. In 1934, the government's Works Project Administration commissioned twenty-five artists to paint the lobby. They were each paid $94 a month. The scenes offer broad interpretations of life in modern California. There are views of the city's bustling Financial

District as well as images of farms, ports and factories from the farther reaches of California.

Although the styles and themes of each mural vary greatly, together they offer an incisive vision of Depression-era America. The commentaries were perhaps a bit too politically incisive, in fact, and when the murals were finished, they caused quite a stir. Before city authorities would unveil the works, several images had to be removed. Communist iconography—a hammer and sickle, for example— proved too much for a city already burdened by bloody labor strikes.

Despite this censorship, the murals are an outstanding work of public art that was created by several acclaimed artists. Bernard Zakheim's *Library* should be especially noted: one of the controversial images that slipped by the censors is a worker's hand reaching for a copy of Karl Marx's infamous manifesto *Das Kapital*. Another is Victor Arnautoff's *City Life*, a detailed portrait of downtown San Francisco that shows a man being mugged at gunpoint amidst a throng of indifferent passersby.

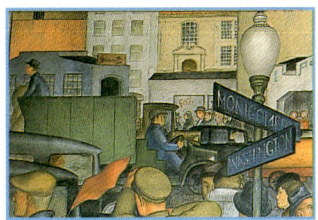

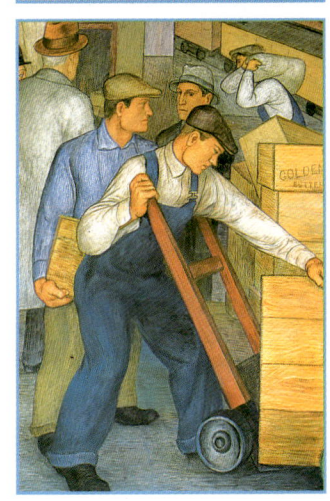

The famous murals in the lobby of Coit Tower date back to the Great Depression.

Filbert and Greenwich Steps — After years of plunder, the east side of Telegraph Hill became quite a sheer cliff indeed. For years when the city was first developing—and even into the twentieth century—dirt was constantly being taken from the hill. At first this dirt was used as ballast for the empty cargo hulls of Gold Rush ships, and later it was used as landfill for the city's ever-expanding downtown area. In any event, what was left of the hill's eastern face was not easily traversed. The Filbert and Greenwich steps, the pedestrian extensions of the two streets, are the best and most scenic way to tackle the hill. Over the course of thirty years a local resident, Grace Merchant, was responsible for transforming the Filbert steps from a dump heap into the beautiful, meandering landscape we see today. The homes along both stairs are some of the city's finest and most expensive, due in large part to the stunning views.

RUSSIAN HILL

With a maximum elevation of 294 feet, Russian Hill affords some of the most impressive views in the city. It is primarily a residential district that has an unusual mix of denizens. While real estate is expensive, the population maintains a somewhat bohemian flavor. As one of the most prestigious residential districts, Russian Hill has some of the premiere residential architecture. The streets are lined with beautiful homes, many in full Victorian splendor. Russian Hill purportedly got its name when the graves of Russian fur traders were discovered at the hill's summit in 1850, when the hill was still largely uninhabited. Houses were generally built at the base of the hill until 1880, when the Union Street cable-car line made Russian Hill more accessible. Telegraph Hill, North Beach and the expansive Bay can be surveyed from many points along **Vallejo Street**. *On the west side of Russian Hill, Vallejo crests at Jones Street, providing an incredible panorama that can be taken in while driving along some pretty scenery. If traveling by foot, the* **Vallejo Street Stairway** *begins at Mason Street and climbs up through Ina Coolbrith Park. Higher still above Taylor Street are several blocks of picturesque Victorian houses. The summit of Russian Hill was one of the few areas in the city not wiped out by the catastrophe of 1906; some of the city's oldest and quaintest houses, therefore, are found here.*

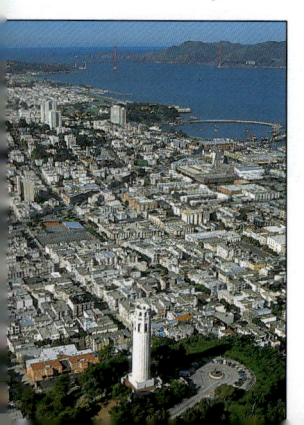

Lombard Street — Hailed as the "crookedest street in the world," the single block of Lombard Street at the summit of Russian Hill includes eight sharp curves. For many years the hill's cobblestoned, twenty-seven-degree natural incline proved too steep for most vehicles to climb. Then in 1922 this block between Hyde and Leavenworth was revamped and the curves were added. Carl Henry, a city entrepreneur with several properties along the block, was the first to propose the corkscrew design. The block was subsequently designed with a sixteen percent grade beautified with a fancy bankment of garden planters. Today traffic flows downhill and there is a pedestrian stairway as well. The homes along this block are quite attractive and well maintained; all were built since 1940.

San Francisco Art Institute — Founded in 1871, the San Francisco Art Institute is the oldest art school on the West Coast and remains one of the top art training centers in the country. The impressive building, a Spanish Colonial-style "monastery" with a medieval concrete tower and a serene interior courtyard surrounded by an architrave, was built in 1926 by San Francisco architects Bakewell & Brown after the institute moved from its perch on Nob Hill.
The institute's **Diego Rivera Gallery** should not be missed. Rivera briefly taught at the institute in the early 1930s, and his large mural in the gallery honors the American Worker. William Lewis Gerstle sponsored the mural, and his personage is portrayed in the man wearing the black hat.

29 Russell Street — According to many, 29 Russell Street is one of the most important residences in San Francisco history. From this unpossessing, brown-shingled cottage sprang the creative genesis of the Beat generation. 29 Russell was the home of Neal and Carolyn Cassady, who in 1952 offered their attic to a drifter named Jack Kerouac. It was here that Kerouac, who become the paramount Beat culture icon, wrote his three major works, *On The Road*, *Visions of Cody* and *Doctor Sax*.

Opposite, aerial view of Telegraph Hill and Russian Hill.
Below, Lombard Street, the "crookedest street in the world."

NOB HILL

In the late 1870s, Robert Louis Stevenson remarked that Nob Hill was "the hill of palaces." The description was fitting over a century ago, and it is fitting now for entirely different reasons. After the invention of the cable car in 1873, the hill became a suburb of sorts, a place where the affluent could stretch out and build grandiose mansions away from the tumult of the city. All but one of the original mansions would be wiped out in 1906, of course, but new palaces would emerge.
The new palaces are not private mansions, but rather luxury hotels, exclusive clubs, an inspiring cathedral and upscale apartments and condominiums that house some of the city's wealthiest tenants.

The Fairmont Hotel — One of the city's most elegant landmarks, The Fairmont Hotel has a storied history indeed. The hotel was built on a block of land owned by Comstock millionaire James Graham Fair, whose fortunes were made mining a fifty-foot vein of silver in the Nevada hills. The hotel, named after the mining magnate, was built by Fair's daughter, Theresa Alice, who commissioned James and Merritt Reid to design the beautiful, 600-room Beaux Arts hotel in 1902. Theresa Alice's husband, Hermann Oeirichs, oversaw the building's construction.

Just before the hotel was completed in 1906, medicine millionaires Herbert and Hartland Law bought the property from Fair. Mere months later, on April 18, the earth-

The Fairmont Hotel, one of the most elegant in San Francisco.

quake struck the city; fire gutted the building the following morning, days before it was scheduled to open. The steel-frame, terra-cotta-clad façade withstood the fire, however, and rebuilding began almost immediately. Theresa Alice Oeirichs offered to buy back the property, and the Laws jumped at the chance to be rid of the charred monolith. Julia Morgan was then enlisted to refurbish the hotel and—amazingly—it opened to the public on the first anniversary of the quake. The gala celebration held on opening day was legendary.

Equally legendary is the building's plush interior. Golden marble columns distinguish the lobby, which Dorothy Draper redecorated in 1947 and which has since remained a paragon of post-war elegance. **The Cirque Bar** around the corner is decorated with large, playful murals painted against a gold-leaf background. In 1962, architect Mario Gaidano added a twenty-two-story tower with an exterior glass elevator that wisks passengers to the **Fairmont Crown** lounge, the highest observation point in the city.

Grace Cathedral — Fifty-three years in the making, Grace Cathedral was finally consecrated in 1964. Today it is the seat of the Episcopal bishop of California. The neo-Gothic cathedral was designed by Lewis P. Hobbart, who was trained at the Ecole des Beaux Arts in Paris. Not coinci-

The neo-Gothic Grace Cathedral.

dentally, the building was modeled after thirteenth-century French cathedrals, most notably Notre Dame.

The cathedral sits on an entire block donated by renowned city benefactor Charles Crocker. When the earthquake leveled his son's mansion in 1906, Crocker gave the space to the church.

The cathedral does a good job filling the lot: it is 329 feet long, 162 feet wide, and each twin belfry towers 174 feet to the heavens. One of the most spectacular aspects of the cathedral is the east entrance, where copies of Lorenzo Ghiberti's bronze *Doors of Paradise* hang. The original doors—made from the same mold—embellish the Baptistry in Florence, Italy.

Inside, the stained-glass windows are transcendent. There are sixty-seven of them, the most impressive being the twenty-five-foot rose window over the entrance. Made in 1964 at the Gabriel Loire studio near Chartres, France, the *Canticle of the Sun* depicts St. Francis of Assisi's spiritual revelation. Behind the altar along the central apse, Charles Jay Connick's lovely 1931 windows portray *Christ the Light of the World* and *Christ the Good Shepherd* in brilliant shades of blue.

Mark Hopkins International Hotel — The Mark Hopkins Hotel, a.k.a. "The Mark," has enjoyed world renown ever since its creation in 1926. The building was designed by the architecture firm Weeks & Day, and it sits on the location of the former Mark Hopkins mansion, which was consumed by fire in 1906. In its glory, the redwood, gingerbread mansion had been the most spectacular Victorian ensemble in California.

The Weeks & Day building, a brick and terra-cotta-clad Gothic Revival design, was created in many ways to commemorate the old gabled castle.

The luxurious brick-paved plaza and the grand pillars at the entrance are equalled by the plush amenities inside. In 1939, the nineteenth floor was remodeled by Timothy Pfleuger and made into a cocktail lounge known far and wide as the **Top of the Mark**. This glassed-in skyroom has 360-degree views of the Bay and surrounding hills and has been the playground of countless celebrities over the years.

Huntington Hotel — Built in 1924 and designed by Weeks & Day, the Huntington Hotel is one of the city's best-loved. This small, 140-room hotel stands at the very peak of Nob Hill and every room has a view of either the Bay or the city below.

The Huntington was designed as a residential hotel, and it still feels rather homey. No two rooms are alike, and the milieu is elegant, charming, quaint and—most importantly—understated. There are no ostentatious displays here, no fuss. The staff is known for the longevity of its employment as well as its discretion.

Pacific-Union Club — A very private bastion of San Francisco's old-guard patriarchy, the Pacific-Union Club was formed in 1881 and remains one of the most exclusive men's social clubs in the country. The dark Connecticut brownstone building, known as the Flood mansion, was bought for $900,000 from mining magnate James Flood after the 1906 fire badly damaged the property. Londoner Augustus Laver—who won the competition to design City Hall in 1887 only to have it destroyed in the earthquake—designed Flood's Italianate, $1.5 million mansion in 1886. Because the building was made of stone and not wood, it was the only structure on Nob Hill to remain standing after the great fire. Nevertheless, it was wholly gutted, and the Flood clan subsequently migrated to Pacific Heights. The original Victorian bronze fence and gates around the property remain some of the city's finest metalwork.
Architect Willis Polk, one of the 450 club members, designed the building's post-fire renovation. The third story and both wings were added and the tower was lowered. In the basement, a luxurious private room was designed with Minoan columns and an illuminated, stained-glass ceiling.

Ritz Carlton Hotel — A babe in the woods among Nob Hill's old-time hotels, the Ritz Carlton has nevertheless asserted itself quite handsomely since its opening in 1991. Already this hotel has established itself as one of the city's

The Ritz Carlton Hotel.

The Cable Car Museum is a spectacle of mechanical ingenuity. Right, a car in the museum.

finest. The hotel is housed in a beautiful, 1909 Beaux Arts building that fills an entire block on California Street, near the summit of the hill. There are 336 impeccably groomed rooms and all the amenities one could desire.

Stouffer Stanford Court Hotel — In the late 1850s, Dr. Arthur Hayne climbed a steep and treacherous hill in San Francisco's hinterlands and built his bride a home. Much history transpired between then and now. The neighborhood would eventually be known as Nob Hill, of course, and where the house once stood is now the impeccable Stouffer Stanford Court Hotel. In the interim, railroad tycoon Leland Stanford built an expansive wooden mansion on the site that was quickly swallowed in the 1906 conflagration. A thirty-foot-tall, dark granite retaining wall along Powell Street is all that remains of the old building. Ironically, Stanford's California Street cable cars still climb the hill and pass by the vanished mansion.

A glorious apartment building designed by Creighton Withers rose from the ashes in 1911. In 1972, the building's interior was completely renovated by Curtis and Davis and quickly became one of the city's grandest hotels. The lobby of the 402-room hotel features a 1992 sepia mural painted by Mark Evans and Charley Brown that shows how the Stanford mansion looked on the hill before its destruction. The beautiful central courtyard and fountain are covered by a towering stained-glass canopy.

Cable Car Museum — The mighty engines that pull the city's cable cars along their routes are found in the Cable Car Museum, which still hums with power all day long. The barn houses the mechanisms that make the cable cars go: purring engines power huge, fourteen-foot sheaves that wind the cables, pulling the cars along their tracks. Being inside the museum and watching the dynamo churn feels like being inside an enormous clock.

The barn was first constructed in 1887 and then rebuilt in 1906 after the quake badly damaged the structure. When the cable-car system was renovated during the 1980s, the barn was reinforced but the exterior was left alone. An underground viewing room shows how the cables loop in and out below street level. The museum also houses three vintage cable cars as well as displays that describe the cars' grip and braking mechanisms in full detail. Photographs and scale models document all the cars that ever grappled a San Francisco hill.

Examples of a cable car grip mechanism. Bottom, a detail of a mechanism.

South Park ◆ 68

San Francisco Museum of Modern Art ◆ 64

Yerba Buena Gardens ◆ 63

Moscone Convention Center ◆ 62

Old Mint Museum ◆ 67

Basic Brown ◆ 73

Levi Strauss & Company ◆ 72

Mission Dolores (the cemetery) ◆ 70

Mission Dolores Basilica, stained-glass ◆ 71

24th Street, Galeria de la Raza ◆ 72

60

SECTION THREE

SOUTH OF MARKET AND THE MISSION

MOMA, *Woman with a hat* by Henry Matisse
◆ 65

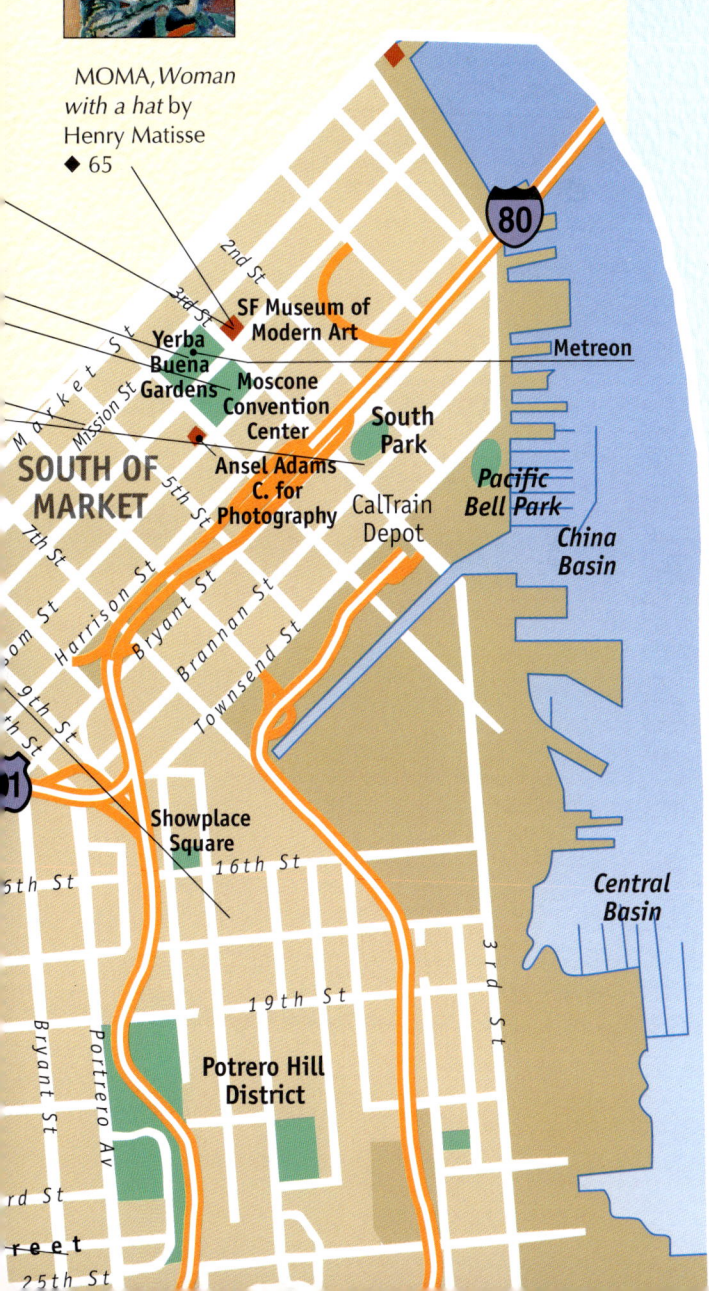

SOUTH OF MARKET

SOMA, the area South of Market Street, is the city's most eclectic neighborhood. Back in the 1850s, before the advent of the cable car lured the affluent to Nob Hill to build their mansions, Rincon Hill was one of the most prestigious addresses in the city. Beginning in 1883, however, Market Street became one of the main cable-car thoroughfares and, in the process, became a distinct social dividing line. The area "South of the Slot," as the cable conduit on Market was known, became an increasingly working-class neighborhood, while the region to the north developed into a solid middle- and upper-class neighborhood. After the 1906 quake leveled the area south of Market, factories, train yards and warehouses were constructed. For the next seventy years, SOMA remained industrial and rather oppressive. Industry eventually moved away, however, and in the 1970s and 1980s artists and musicians began to convert the large factory spaces into studios and living quarters. The area has gotten progressively more gentrified ever since. Today the area has a world-class cultural center, a spiffy new museum, a convention center, trendy restaurants, bars and clubs, a flower market and several popular retail outlets, not to mention attractive new residential developments.

Moscone Convention Center — San Francisco's primary convention hall, the Moscone Center occupies an entire city block and boasts over one million square feet of useable space. Designed by Hellmuth, Obata and Kassabaum in 1981, the convention center is the centerpiece of the Yerba Buena Gardens project. It was named after Mayor George Moscone, who was assassinated by disgruntled ex-supervisor Dan White on November 28, 1978. The subterranean exhibit hall covers 300,000 square feet and is an impressive architectural feet. Engineered by T.Y. Lin, the hall boasts an astounding system of supports that makes interior columns unnecessary. Incredibly, the arched roof is supported by a network of steel cables that runs under the floor. The result is a vast, expansive space, one of the largest underground spaces in the world. Despite being largely underground, the convention center employs an imaginative array of skylights and artificial lights that prevent the space from seeming a gaping, dark cave. In 1988, Anthony Lumsden of DMJM and Gensler & Associates designed a rooftop reception hall and another underground meeting space that cost $200 million and effectively doubled the size of the facility.

Opposite: a view of Yerba Buena Gardens, where SFMOMA stands in the distance.

Yerba Buena Gardens — Thirty years in the planning, the Yerba Buena Center project was begun to promote the city's diverse artistic community. Opened in 1993, the $87 million center features several first-rate facilities, including the **Visual Arts Center**, **Yerba Buena Gardens** and the **Esplanade**. The Visual Arts Center is the first work in the United States designed by cutting-edge Japanese architect Fumihiko Maki. The façade is dark and industrial-looking, with sections of corrugated metal siding. Inside the center offers 55,000 square feet of gallery space and a sculpture court that exhibit contemporary art. Across the way, **Yerba Buena Theater** was designed by New York architect James Stewart Polshek and features a 750-seat theater reserved for the use of nonprofit companies. There is also an outdoor stage with lawn seating that can accommodate 3,000. Between the arts center and the theater, the Esplanade unifies the whole Yerba Buena project. The centerpiece is the **Martin Luther King Memorial,** a twenty-foot-high, fifty-foot-wide, Sierra granite waterfall designed by sculptor Houston Conwell. Illuminated glass panels are inscribed with the fallen civil rights leader's inspiring words. All around the green lawn there are many activities for kids such as: an ice-skating rink, a bowling alley, a historic **Carousel** from 1906 and the **Zeum**, wich is an interactive cultural center geared specifically for children and teenagers.

Sony Metreon — Four floors and 350,000 square feet of entertainment and countless ways to escape into a whole new reality. The Sony Metreon sits on the Yerba Buena Garden lawn and it's a combination of the best of Sony with the original efforts of artists, architects, animator, chefs, writers, and digital masterminds.

San Francisco Museum of Modern Art — Swiss architect Mario Botta's dazzling San Francisco Museum of Modern Art opened in 1995, becoming the city's premiere monument of contemporary architecture. The new building replaces the former space provided—inadequately—by the Civic Center's Veteran's Building and firmly establishes SFMOMA as a rising star in the international art world. It also has become a cornerstone for the Yerba Buena Gardens project.

Botta's $62 million, 50,000-square-foot building has both power and vision. The five-story structure is clad in burnt-sienna brick and features a 125-foot-tall, black-and-white-striped cylinder cut at a dramatic angle and capped by a brilliant skylight. The center of the façade is marked by a vertical slot that gives the building an intriguing look. The ground floor entrance presents a broad glazed wall. Inside, the sun-filled atrium astounds, rising five floors to the skylight. A grand staircase leads from the atrium to the four floors of spacious galleries.

Front entrance of the San Francisco Museum of Modern Art.

SFMOMA houses some of the world's greatest modern paintings. Top, left and right, Woman with a Hat *and* Girl with Green Eyes, *by Henri Matisse. Right,* Frida and Diego Rivera, *by Frida Kahlo.*

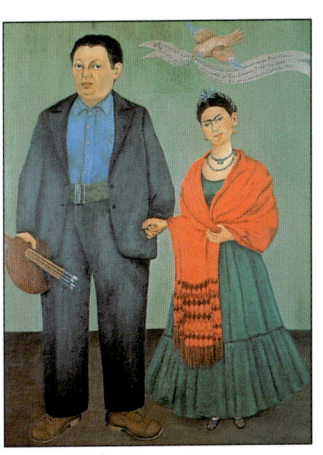

The San Francisco Museum of Art opened in 1935; it didn't become the Museum of Modern Art until forty years later, when it was directed by Harry Hopkins. Today it has over 17,000 pieces of art in many different mediums. Some of the SFMOMA's great modern European paintings include Henri Matisse's *Girl with Green Eyes* and *Woman with a Hat*—probably the museum's most famous possession; Pablo Picasso's *Women of Algiers*; Georges Braque's *Gueridon*; Wassily Kandinsky's *Brownish*; Joan Miró's *Painting*; Georgia O'Keeffe's *Black Place*; Frida Kahlo's *Frida and Diego Rivera* and Diego Rivera's *Flower Carrier*.

There are thirty-five paintings by American Abstract Expressionist Clyfford Still as well as works from many kindred spirits: Jasper Johns, William de Kooning, Philip Guston, Robert Rauschenberg, Frank Stella, Andy Warhol and Roy Lichtenstein. Jackson Pollock's *Guardians of the Secret* is the museum's American Expressionist masterpiece.

In addition to the vast painting and sculpture collection, there are more than 9,000 photographs culled from the ranks of the masters. Walker Evans, Edward Steichen and Alfred Stieglitz are represented, along with Californians

Edward Weston, John Gutmann and Ansel Adams.

The Architecture and Design collection includes over 1,700 objects. California designers and architects steal the show: Bernard Maybeck, Timothy Pflueger, Willis Polk, Charles and Ray Eames, Frank Lloyd Wright and Frank Gehry—all contributors to the city's landscape—are represented here.

There are also separate galleries reserved for California Arts and Media Arts, which provides state-of-the-art viewing equipment. In addition, the fourth and fifth floors are used to display special exhibitions and newly acquired works. About twenty temporary exhibits are featured each year, which does much to encourage the city's contemporary art scene.

SFMOMA, top to bottom: Black Place I, *by Georgia O'Keeffe;* Noel in the kitchen, *by Joan Brown;* Berkeley # 23, *by Richard Diebenkorn.*

Ansel Adams Center for Photography — Opened in 1989, the Ansel Adams Center has quickly become one of the world's outstanding photography showplaces. The center's namesake is famed California photographer Ansel Adams, who was born in San Francisco in 1902 and whose impressionistic landscapes, especially those of the Yosemite Valley, are some of the world's best-known photographs. Before his death in 1984, Adams donated 125 of his works to the Friends of Photography, the association he co-founded in 1967 and which runs the center today.

The modern, converted concrete building across from Yerba Buena Gardens houses five galleries, one of which exhibits Adams's great oeuvre. The center stages about fifteen exhibits a year, which range from one-artist retrospectives to thematic group shows.

Old Mint Museum — Contrary to its name, the Old U.S. Mint was actually the second mint opened in San Francisco. Designed by Alfred Mullet in 1874, the Old U.S. Mint was built in neo-classical style with stately Doric columns lined across the gray granite façade. The Old Mint has a powerful mien, which probably proved useful when the building's vault once housed a third of the nation's gold reserve.

The "Granite Lady," as the building is known, was the only financial institution that survived the cataclysms of 1906 intact, and it was instrumental in the city's relief effort. The minting operation ceased in 1937, and the building was converted into government offices. In 1972, the Treasury Department restored the landmark building as a museum. Today tours of the Old Mint include viewing a million dollars in gold bullion and a collection of antique minting equipment.

The Ansel Adams Center Photography.

A view of South Park.

SOUTH PARK

Once a place of leisure for the wealthy residents of SOMA in the mid-nineteenth century, South Park declined and then rose again with the fate of the neighborhood. The oval-shaped park was built in 1856 with London's Berkeley Square as a model. At that time it was lined with elegant homes and mansions. A mass exodus of the city's affluent to Nob Hill in the 1870s left the area bereft for over a century. Industry moved into the neighborhood and then moved out, leaving only squalor. Construction of the Bay Bridge in the 1930s did yet more injustice to South Park, and only quite recently did it begin to rebound. The arrival of artists to the area followed by the general development of the neighborhood has brought life back to the park. Once again the park's weeping willows and sycamore trees provide shade for the neighborhood's well-to-do.

THE MISSION

A sheltered valley on the fringe of San Francisco, The Mission District was one of the earliest settlements in the Bay Area. When the focus of the city switched to Yerba Buena Cove in the early 1850s, The Mission became something of a suburb. Although settled first by the local Ohlone tribe and then Spanish missionaries, by the end of the nineteenth century it was inhabited largely by Irish immigrants. The area survived the calamities of 1906 in good form, and to this day some of the city's oldest and finest Victorian homes can be found here.

On the left, the front of the Mission Dolores, built in 1791.

Today The Mission is once again largely Hispanic and still feels rather suburban. The streets are wide and the buildings low and—guarded by the hills from the fog rolling in off the Bay—The Mission enjoys the city's finest weather. Cinco de Mayo, which commemorates the victory of Mexican troops over Napolean III's invasion forces in 1862, is the area's most festive celebration. Because rents are generally cheap, The Mission has a strong bohemian culture as well.

Mission Dolores — San Francisco's first mission, Mission Dolores was settled by Spanish clerics led by Captain José Moraga in 1776. The current building was built in 1791, which makes the mission the oldest standing building in the city. Although the mission was originally dedicated to St. Francis of Assisi, it later assumed patronage by Our Lady of Sorrows. Mission Dolores was the sixth of the twenty-one missions founded by Mexicans along El Camino Real, the historic road leading all the way from Mexico to Sonoma, California. The crusade of missionaries was directed by Father Serra, who was beatified by the Roman Catholic Church in 1988.

The mission's four-foot adobe walls have survived four major earthquakes. It is the only one of the original missions that is still standing and has not needed extensive repair. The painted ceilings were patterned after Ohlone tribal basket designs, and all the decorations, including the

Interior of the Basilica, built in 1913, wich towers over the adjacent Mission Dolores; top, a detail of the façade.

statues, altars and bells, were carried from Mexico along El Camino Real by packs of mules. Behind the mission is a picturesque old cemetery with the remains of some of the city's earliest pioneers and settlers. Included are over 5,000 members of the Ohlone tribe who were wiped out by measles in the early 1800s

24th Street — Along 24th Street from Mission to Bryant is the heart of the Latino shopping and restaurant district. The Mission has one of the West Coast's most complex Latino communities, and 24th Street caters largely to them. As a result of various civil wars in Central and South America, many Latino immigrants have settled in The Mission and opened up shop. There are Spanish-speaking Nicaraguan, Costa Rican and Salvadoran restaurants and specialty stores. Markets provide exotic tropical fruits and vegetables. The ambience is very much Latino in flavor.

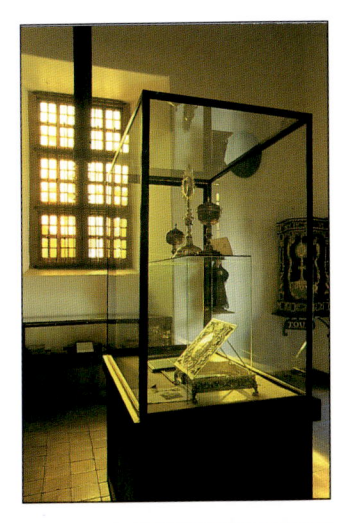

Ancient artifacts preserved inside the little museum of the Mission Dolores.

A stained-glass' detail from the Mission Dolores Basilica.

Outdoor Murals — Visually, The Mission is known for its colorful streets and especially its outdoor murals, which depict Latino political and cultural ideas. Focused in the area bound by Mission and York and 14th and Army, these paintings are found on banks, restaurants, schools and community centers throughout the neighborhood. In the late 1960s, Chicano murals first emerged in the *barrios* of East Los Angeles and then spread to the Bay Area.

At the southeast corner of 22nd Street and South Van Ness stands one of the most well-known of these murals, *Inspire to Aspire: Tribute to Carlos Santana*, painted by Michael Rios, Carlos Gonzalez and Johnny Mayorga and funded by the city in 1987. This fanciful mural portrays Latino musicians against a background that includes both an ancient Aztec pyramid and the current San Francisco skyline.

Painted by Daniel Galvez in 1984, *Golden Dream of the*

New World is another fine mural at 24th Street and South Van Ness. Here Latin dancers are shown against a background of rainbow-painted Victorian houses. More politically militant, the **Balmy Street murals** on the south side of 24th Street were begun in 1973 by a community group of some forty artists. The themes here depict scenes of political upheaval common throughout Central America.

Galeria de la Raza — Founded in 1970, the nonprofit Galeria de la Raza exhibits the works of local Hispanic artists. The gallery has achieved international recognition for promoting the contemporary arts of the Latino community. The adjoining Studio 24 supports the gallery space by selling traditional and contemporary Mexican and Central American folk art and Latin American literature.

Levi Strauss & Company — The world's oldest and most famous blue-jean company, Levi Strauss has occupied its factory on Valencia Street since the 1906 earthquake. In 1970 the factory was given a face-lift by Howard Friedman, who designed the building's Western plains, cowboy look. The factory offers a forty-five minute tour with short film that chronicles the history of Levi jeans. The Levi Strauss Playground in front of the building was donated to the city by philanthropist Rosalie Stern.

The trade-mark of Levi Strauss & Company.

The mural Golden Dream of the New World.

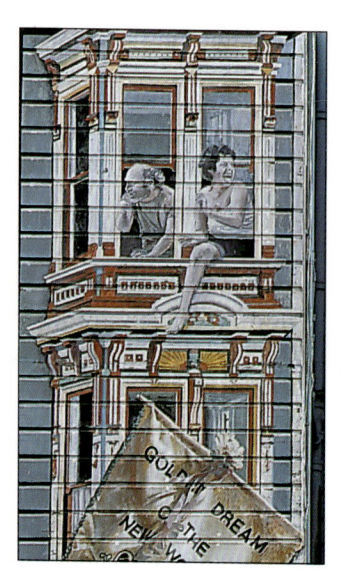

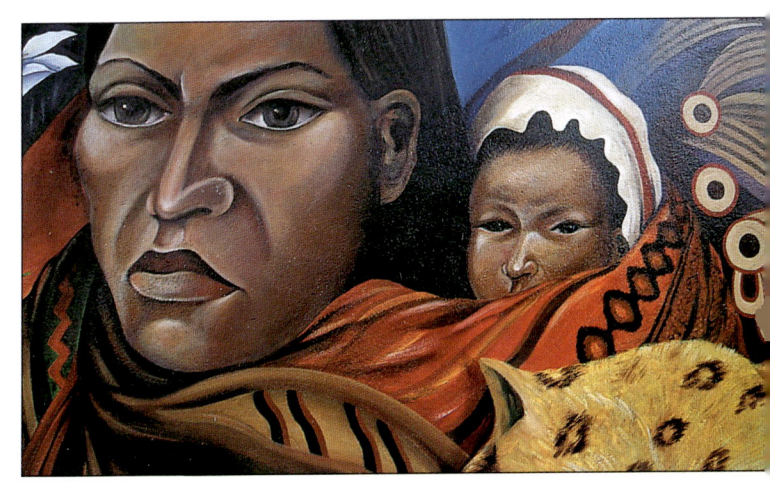

A mural in Potrero District.

POTRERO HILL DISTRICT

A quiet, sleepy residential district, Potrero Hill overlooks The Mission District to the west and downtown San Francisco to the north. Like The Mission, Potrero Hill was an early suburb, joined to the city by a five-mile stretch of cable-car tracks. The area enjoys the city's sunniest climate and sports some lovely colorful houses. It has now become home to many good restaurants and shops. Among the neighborhood's claims to fame, Vermont Street is nearly as curvaceous as Russian Hill's Lombard Street—but the turns are even more hair-raising and heart-stopping. Anchor Steam Brewery on Mariposa Street, founded in 1851 to quench gold diggers' thirsts, is the city's choice beer maker.

Basic Brown Bears — Sure to please all small children, Basic Brown Bears is a small stuffed-animal factory that specializes in—can you guess?—teddy bears. The factory offers a free thirty minute tour, after which shoppers can buy and stuff their own loveable teddy bears.

Showplace Square — At the foot of Potrero Hill among a host of other restored nineteenth-century warehouses stands Showplace Square, one of the largest wholesale furniture centers in the country. Open to the trade, these showrooms offer furniture and interior decoration in just about every conceivable style. The **Design Center** within the square consists of two warehouses linked by a modern, glass atrium used for exhibitions and conventions.

SECTION FOUR

THE HAIGHT AND THE CASTRO

Haight-Ashbury
◆ 77

Twin Peaks
◆ 75

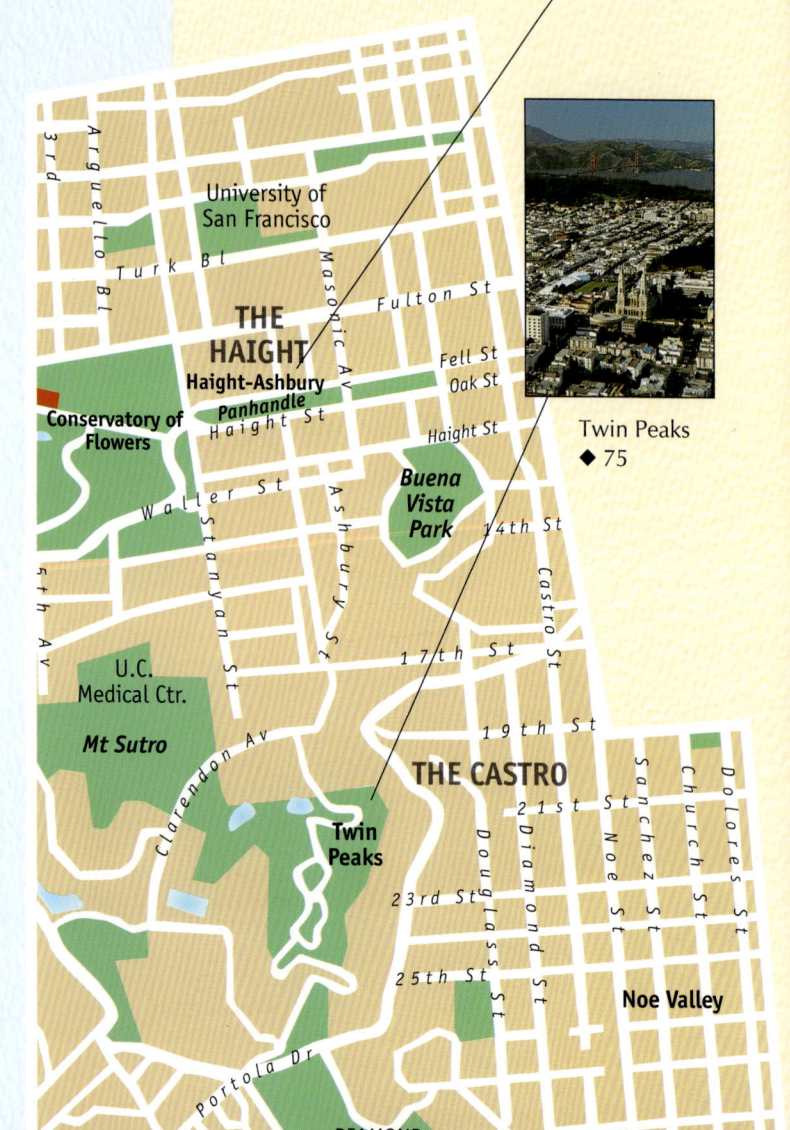

View of downtown San Francisco from Twin Peaks.

TWIN PEAKS

Once known as Los Pechos de la Chola, The Breasts of the Indian Girl, the Twin Peaks are the city's second- and third-tallest hills, both topping 900 feet. The 360-degree views from the top of Twin Peaks are incredible, especially at night when the lights of the city are ablaze below. When Daniel Burnham needed a look-out post from which to survey and plan the city in 1905, he came to Twin Peaks. Today Twin Peaks is a residential district with some of the city's largest properties. There is a bit more elbow room here, and many of the homes have gardens and lush landscaping. Twin Peaks Boulevard wraps around both hills and offers some great vistas.

NOE VALLEY

Noe Valley is a self-sufficient community, quite indifferent to the goings-on downtown. At the border of the Mission District and the Haight Ashbury, Noe Valley is a comfy neighborhood and a pleasant place to stroll around without being in a touristy area. It's an engaging mixture of eclectic shops and coffeehouses. The area was named after José de Jesus Noe, the last Mexican mayor of the city then known as Yerba Buena. Today there is a bohemian element, once compared to New York's Greenwich Village, as well as a young, professional contingent that arrived in the 1970s, when downtown real estate became unaffordable. 24th Street has all the commercial interests any small city could offer, and the Victorian homes are homey and well-kept. The neighborhood has a remarkable small-town feel.

THE HAIGHT

The Haight district comprises several diverse social communities, including those of Golden Gate Park, Buena Vista Hill and the legendary Haight-Ashbury neighborhood. The physical landscape is as variegated as the population, as grand mansions often rub shoulders with run-down townhouses. Developed later than the other neighborhoods on the fringe of the city, the Haight was lucky to rise in the Victorian splendor of the 1890s. The **Panhandle**, the narrow, eight-block stretch of park along Oak Street, was intended as a carriage entry to Golden Gate Park. Like the rest of the neighborhood, it was lined with stately Victorian homes, many of which still stand today with brand new coats of paint.

The neighborhood's decline began in 1917, however, when construction of the Twin Peaks tunnel lured denizens of the Haight out to the more secluded and spacious city limits. This trend of decay persisted through the 1950s. In the 1960s, low

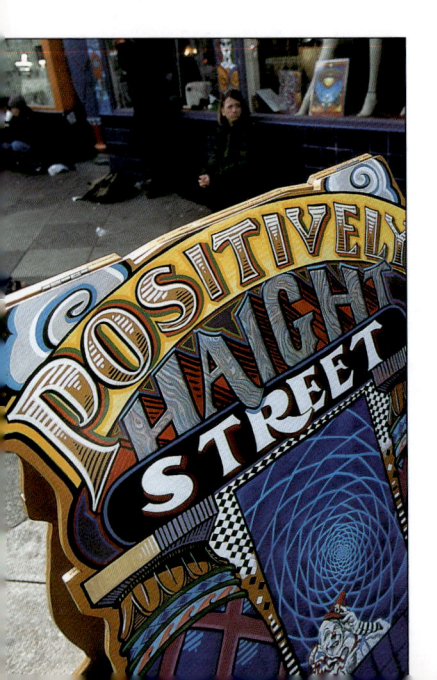

A sign in Haight Street.

rents and good karma attracted infamous hordes of hippies to the neighborhood, which became the mecca of the entire Love Generation. The decline of the Haight continued. Only in the past decade has the Haight been reborn, undergoing vast gentrification. Today the Haight is home to many young, middle- and upper-class professionals.

Haight-Ashbury — In 1967, the Summer of Love transformed the dilapidated neighborhood known as Haight-Ashbury. 200,000 young people pilgrimaged to Haight-Ashbury that summer, lured by the promise of peace, love and understanding. Those brief three months would define an entire generation as well as the neighborhood where that generation was born.

Secluded by surrounding parkland and mired in glorious decay, Haight-Ashbury was a perfect place to launch the hippie revolution. Kids came to act against the Establishment and to indulge their wildest dreams of communal living, drugs, sex and music. This small community nurtured some of the most legendary rock musicians of all time: the Grateful Dead rested their heads at **710 Ashbury Street**; Janis Joplin resided at **122 Lyon Street**; Jefferson Airplane took off from **2400 Fulton Street**. When the party was finally over in the 1970s and the last guests had trickled out, Haight-Ashbury had a lot of cleaning up to do. Now the neighborhood is on the rise again, the home to a solidly established professional class.

THE CASTRO

The Castro proudly boasts the city's largest gay population. Perhaps nowhere else in the world do gay men wield such political might and enjoy such broad social acceptance. Castro Street is the main thoroughfare, lined with restaurants, bars, cafes, stores and boutiques that openly cater to the gay community. The neighborhood's biggest celebrations are the Gay Freedom Day parade in June and the Halloween extravaganza, which brings out all the ghouls and goblins on October 31. The Castro is a stylish and well-maintained neighborhood that does a good job assimilating modern architecture into the Victorian landscape.

Golden Gate Bridge ◆ 84

Cliff House ◆ 82

Golden Gate Bridge
Fort Point
Golden Promer
Pet Cem

MILE ROCK

Baker Beach

THE PRESIDI

South Bay

Land's End

China Beach

California St

Seal Rocks

Lincoln Park

California Palace of the Legion of Honor

Point Lobos Av

Cliff House

The Presidio ◆ 80

San Francisco National Maritime Museum ◆ 94

Mari Green
Marina
Palace of Fine Arts
Richardson Av
Filbert
Union
Vallejo
Broderick St
Backer St
Lyon St
Jackson St
Washington St

Palace of Fine Arts ◆ 89

Embarcadero Center ◆ 105

78

SECTION FIVE

THE WATERFRONT

Fisherman's Wharf ◆ 92

Alcatraz ◆ 98

Pier 39 ◆ 93

The Presidio Army Museum and, bottom, an ornate cannon.

THE PRESIDIO

The Presidio was founded by the Spanish in 1776 to guard the entrance to San Francisco Bay. The original installation was a hundred-yard-square camp surrounded by a palisade wall. When the Mexicans gained independence in 1822, they took over the site. When the United States annexed California in 1846, the Presidio became a U.S. military base. When the base was recently closed, it had been the longest-serving military *base in the country. Union soldiers trained here during the Civil War, and during World War II it was a significant army headquarters. Planted with pine and eucalyptus trees in the 1880s, the 1,446-acre Presidio includes the largest tract of forest in the city, the majority of which is part of the* **Golden Gate National Recreation Center**. *Unspoiled nature is the big draw here today, as beautiful sprawling paths cut through the forest and offer panoramic views. The Presidio is to become the largest urban National Park in the United States.*

The Presidio Army Museum — Built in 1863 and formerly the Old Station Hospital, the Army Museum is the oldest surviving building in the Presidio. The museum is surrounded by defunct artillery. Inside is a vast collection of memorabilia recounting the army's history in the Bay Area, including old uniforms and weapons, portraits and early photographs, wartime propaganda and strategic maps and charts. The museum has a strong bent towards the nineteenth century, when the army played an important role in taming the West.

Pet Cemetery — Tucked away off Crissy Field Avenue behind a quaint white picket fence, the pet cemetery that has proliferated in recent years was originally reserved for military animals and pets only. Civilians have apparently infringed upon the picturesque setting to lay their four-legged loved ones to rest, sharing these sacred grounds with such courageous national heroes as General Pershing's horse.

The Military Cemetery in the Presidio is the final resting site for many American soldiers.

Cliff House — A mere shadow of its former self, the Cliff House today houses a restaurant that sheds little light on the building's storied past. The original Cliff House was built back in 1863 as a ocean-side retreat for the city's affluent. Over the years the resort became a reputed mob hang out. On Christmas Day in 1894, the building burned down. The following year, Comstock millionaire Adolph Sutro built a Gothic wooden castle on the sight and opened it as a family resort. Next to the building he opened the **Sutro Baths**, a three-acre spa reminiscent of the bathhouses of ancient Rome. Sutro's bathhouse included six saltwater swimming pools beneath a beautiful colored-glass canopy. Unfortunately, Sutro's wondrous castle burned down within a year, and the baths followed suit in 1966. The current building was built in 1909, although recent remodeling has claimed that building's charm as well. Although the bathhouse is in ruins today—an algae-covered swamp—there is talk of renovating the entire complex.

At any rate, the **Seal Rocks** remain. Four hundred feet off the coast of the Cliff House, the rocks swarm with barking sea lions, a sound that can be either playful or eerie, depending on the fog cover.

California Palace of the Legion of Honor — From its hilltop perch in the Presidio, the Legion of Honor holds a commanding view of the city and the Golden gate Bridge spanning the bay. However stunning, the view is no more impressive than the building itself, a French-style palace designed by George Applegarth in 1916. Using the Palais de la Légion d'Honneur in Paris as a model, Applegarth designed the building with grand colonnades and a very triumphal arch. The building was donated by Mr. and Mrs. Adolph Spreckels in 1924 to commemorate Californian soldiers lost in World War I. The Palace of the Legion of Honor was completely renovated and reopened in 1995.

Outside, the museum has several notable statues, including two Rodin masterpieces, *The Thinker* and *The Shades*, which foreshadow the delights of the Rodin Gallery inside, where over seventy of his works are displayed. The museum was devoted exclusively to French art until the early 1990s, when the M.H. de Young Museum donated a vast European collection. The museum's present holdings span eight centuries through the early twentieth century and include paintings, sculptures and decorative arts. Among the early masters whose works hang here are Rubens, Rembrandt, Van Dyck and El Greco; later masters include Degas, Cézanne, Seurat, Renoir, Manet and Monet. Period rooms beautifully capture long-lost times and places. Downstairs the museum holds the largest collection of graphic prints in the West. All told, in both presentation and content, the Legion of Honor is splendid.

Baker Beach — Baker Beach is better for fishing than for swimming, but the mile-long stretch is a nice place to relax and have a picnic. The concrete bunkers on the beach were built to defend the Golden Gate Bridge from attack during World War II. Although the guns have been removed, the evocative bunkers still suggest a lingering, ominous threat.

China Beach — A favorite among locals, China Beach is one of the few city beaches where swimming is permitted. The small beach is protected by a cove that makes the water relatively safe for swimming, but can do nothing to make it less frigid. The beach was named after the Chinese fishermen who used to camp here in days of yore.

Fort Point — A thrilling Civil War relic, Fort Point resides under the southern arch of the Golden Gate Bridge. The fort was built by Union forces between 1853 and 1861 to protect the entrance of San Francisco Bay. The staunch, massive brick fort was built a mere ten feet above the encroaching sea, lending the building a courageous and defiant attitude. Although the fort was furnished with 126 cannons and a vast arsenal, not a single shot was ever fired from here in defense of the city.
The fort's thick walls are built around a vaulted-brick courtyard that is accessed through monolithic, studded doors. Inside are living quarters and a garrison that have been converted into a museum featuring vintage photographs, uniforms and weapons. The parapets facing the bay, usually braced by cold, stiff winds, offer an incredible view of the Golden Gate Bridge above and the city behind.

A view from above of the Cliff House.

Fort Point, built to protect the bay during the Civil War of 1861.

GOLDEN GATE BRIDGE

San Francisco's most powerful icon, the Golden Gate Bridge is arguably the most beautiful bridge in the world. Spanning a beautiful land and seascape bound by the hills of Marin on one side and the Presidio on the other, the bridge is also remarkable for its graceful lines, unique color, Moderne accents and even the sublime, evocative currents of fog that often obscure it.
Joseph Strauss was chief engineer of the project and Clif-

One of California's most awesome views: San Francisco Bay and Golden Gate Bridge, taken from the Marin foothills.

ford Paine supervised construction, which was begun in 1933 and finished four years later. The total cost of the project was $35 million; that sum was finally paid off by bridge tolls in 1971. Before construction began, there were many protests against the project, which would greatly alter the natural landscape at the mouth of the bay. When the 4,200-foot span was completed, however, there were few nay-sayers.

Until New York's Verrazzano Bridge was built in 1959, the Golden Gate was the longest continuous bridge span in the world. The roadway hovers 260 feet above the water, while the art-deco towers rise yet another 486 feet.

The suspension cables that keep the bridge aloft are over thirty-six inches wide. Midway across, the bridge was built to sway up to twenty-seven feet in high winds or earthquakes, which certainly doesn't alleviate pedestrian vertigo. Walkways were included in the design of the bridge, offering spectacular views; the one-way hike is about 1.2 miles. The Golden Gate Bridge is the most photographed man-made structure in the world.

When the Golden Gate Bridge was completed in 1937, it was the longest continuous bridge span in the world.

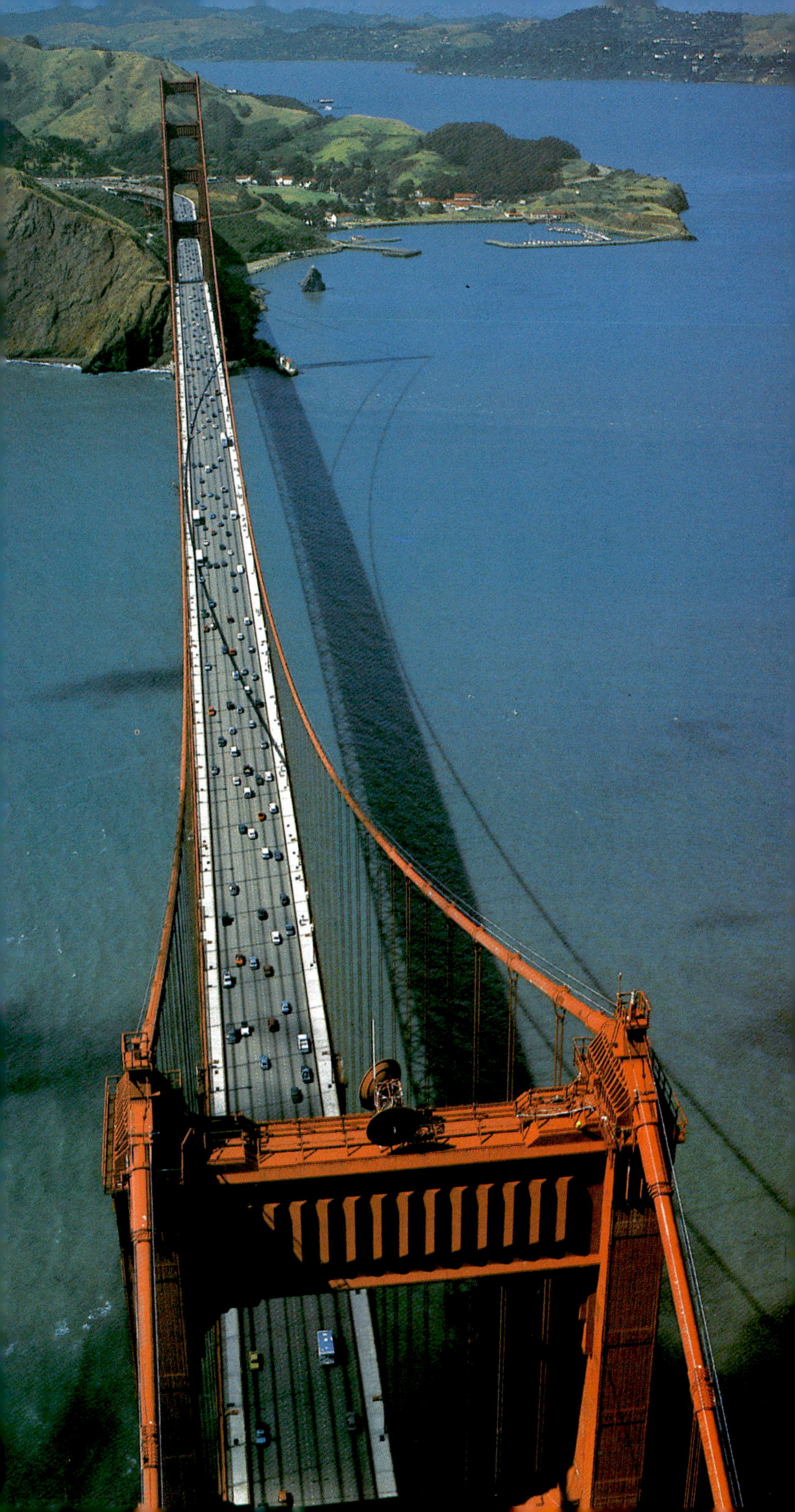

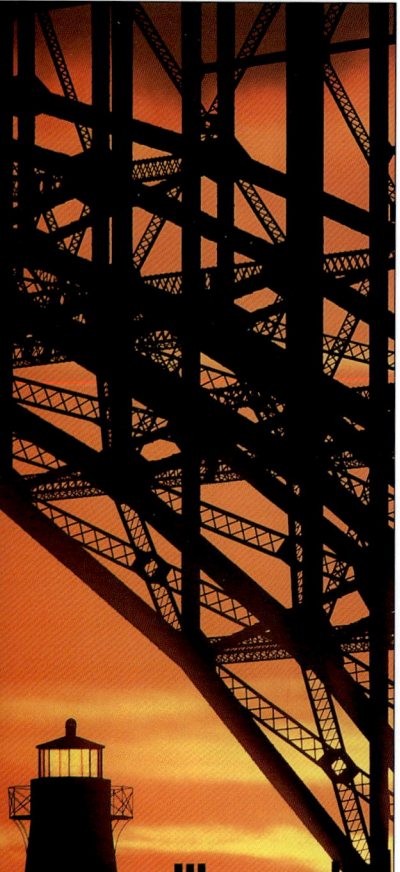

Night views of San Francisco and the Golden Gate Bridge.

THE MARINA

The Marina District is a flat residential neighborhood built largely on landfill, which accounts for its poor showing in the 1989 Loma Prieta earthquake. Much Marina housing was damaged in that quake and several homes were subsequently lost to fire. The Marina and SOMA, in fact, were the neighborhoods hardest hit by Loma Prieta. Nevertheless, the Marina has rebounded from the quake and has again been restored to a quiet, affluent, pastel-colored neighborhood. The buildings reflects the Italianate architecture popular in the 1920s, when many of these houses were built.

Marina Green — A narrow park that stretches along the Yacht Harbor with a tremendous bay view, Marina Green is the neighborhood playground. Many residents of this affluent enclave, in fact, have boats docked in front. When not testing their sea legs, locals come to Marina Green to exercise, fly kites, relax and generally see and be seen. The west end of Marina Green features a **wave organ**, a most unusual musical instrument. Best heard at high tide, the organ's jumble of pipes were designed to whine and belch as waves hit it.

Palace of Fine Arts — Designed by architect Bernard Maybeck as the centerpiece of the Panama-Pacific International Exposition of 1915, the Palace of Fine Arts was such a

The Palace of Fine Arts and the Exploratorium Science Museum.

huge success that it was left standing after the Exposition ended. For years the Palace slowly decayed until a city benefactor donated funds to restore it in 1962. The restoration was completed in 1969, the year the **Exploratorium Science Museum** was opened inside the Palace.

The Exposition of 1915 marked the opening of the Panama Canal, but more significantly celebrated the rebirth of the city reduced to rubble and ash in 1906. For that reason Maybeck's triumphal design struck a chord in the hearts of San Franciscans. Set in a lovely park with a duck pond, Maybeck's classical Roman rotunda looms majestically over two Corinthian colonnades. Atop the colonnades are beautifully sculpted weeping maidens and a remarkable entablature cast in high relief.

One of the finest children's science museums in the country, the Exploratorium Museum was founded by Frank Oppenheimer—whose brother Robert invented the atomic bomb—on the premise that one learns by doing. The 650 hands-on exhibits, therefore, all require some degree of visitor participation to reveal the physical wonders of the world. The **Tactile Dome** within the museum creates an intriguing, vacuous environment void of most physical sensations.

Chestnut Street — Between Divisadero and Fillmore, Chestnut Street is the Marina's main shopping street and the new hot spot for young urban professionals to wine and dine. Despite being one of the city's trendiest locales, Chestnut Street remains a rather quaint stretch of restaurants, cafes and boutiques that has so far managed to avoid tacky commercialization. Time may be running out for Chestnut Street, however, as its newfound celebrity threatens its small-town charm.

Detail of the Exploratorium's intricately carved façade.

FORT MASON AND NORTHERN WATERFRONT

Western frontier headquarters for the U.S. army in the mid-nineteenth century and a pivotal command post during World War II, Fort Mason is today one of the city's most important cultural centers. With over fifty cultural organizations spread over this bayside parkland, including several museums, theaters and galleries, Fort Mason has made the transition to civilian life quite smoothly.

The land was originally residential property until Union soldiers took it over in the 1850s to construct an army compound. Seeing the manicured lawns of the **Great Meadow** today, it is hard to imagine that 1.6 million soldiers embarked from Fort Mason to fight in the Pacific during World War II.

The base was demilitarized in 1972, and since then it has become a significant art and cultural mecca. The fort's barracks and warehouses have been converted into an arts complex called the **Fort Mason Center**.

In an effort to promote Latino cultures in the U.S., the **Mexican Museum** here collects and exhibits a broad range of modern and traditional arts of Mexicans and Mexican-Americans. Another well-established resource center, the **African-American Historical and Cultural Society** includes a library and gallery space used to exhibit works by contemporary African-Americans and also to recount the history of African-American pioneers in the Bay Area. Established to celebrate the identity of one of the city's earliest and most prominent ethnic communities, the **Museo Italo-Americano** stages a wide variety of historical and cultural exhibitions. The widely-acclaimed **San Francisco Craft & Folk Art Museum** displays and sells handmade crafts from around the world.

The **San Francisco Museum of Modern Art** rental gallery is also in the park, as is the **San Francisco Maritime Historical Library**. Some of the city's finest experimental theater is staged at Fort Mason as well, and walks along the 3.5-mile **Golden Gate Promenade**, which cuts through the compound along rocky cliffs, are enjoyed by locals and tourists alike.

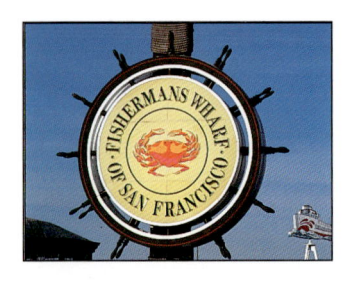

FISHERMAN'S WHARF

*The city's most popular tourist attraction, Fisherman's Wharf was given its carnival façade in the late 1970s and hasn't looked back since. Chinese fishermen first settled here back in the city's earliest days, followed by the Italians in the late nineteenth century. The piers were stocked with colorful boats and the fishing commerce was swift and easy until the mid-twentieth century. After World War II, the bay became increasingly polluted and fishing in northern California became overly competitive. The fishing trade dropped off, and the piers fell into neglect. To reinvigorate the area, the shipping piers and surrounding streets were transformed into a tourist haven. The streets are lined with such thrilling amusements as the **Guinness Museum of World Records** and **Ripley's Believe It or Not! Museum**, making Fisherman's Wharf a gaudy spectacle, but one not to be missed.*

Aerial view of Pier 39 and Fisherman's Wharf.

Pier 39 — The centerpiece of Fisherman's Wharf, Pier 39 was converted into a glitzy, faux-eighteenth-century New England wharf in 1978. After Walt Disney's two fun parks, Pier 39 is the most-visited amusement attraction in the country. The complex includes two levels of shops, restaurants and amusements that cater to every tourist whim. A ride in the **double-deck carousel** is a favorite among young children, as is **Underwater World**, a 50,000-square-foot aquarium that presents a vast array of northern California's indigenous marine life. A high-tech multimedia show, the **San Francisco Experience** gives an

Images from Pier 39. Bottom, barking sea lions frolicking on the pier.

93

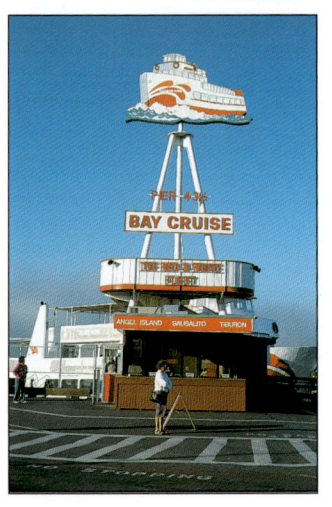

impressive overview of what the city is all about. Although the uninvited horde of barking **sea lions** has become one of the Pier's strongest attractions, the street performers are pretty entertaining as well. The **Blue and Gold Fleet** ferry departs from Pier 39 and gives sight-seeing tours of the bay.

San Francisco National Maritime Museum — The National Maritime Museum captures the essence of San Francisco from its beginnings as a small frontier seaport. Since those early days, the small town has became a major metropolis, but an affinity for the sea has remained. The Maritime Museum chronicles the city's seafaring history with countless pho-

A few of the sights along Fisherman's Wharf.

94

The building of the San Francisco National Maritime Museum.

tographs, nautical instruments and model ship displays. The building itself is remarkable for its ship-shaped, art deco façade that still maintains many of its original 1930s features. Moored nearby at the **Hyde Street Pier** is one of the world's largest collections of old ships, including such tall beauties as the *CA Thayer* and the *Balclutha*.

Balclutha, the historic ship built in 1886.

The Wax Museum — A long-time tourist favorite, the Wax Museum features one of the world's largest collection's of life-size wax figures. The museum portrays the images of such famed historical and fictional characters as Dracula, Al Capone, William Shakespeare, Winston Churchill, Mozart, Elvis Presley, Marilyn Monroe and even the Devil incarnate. There are fourteen U.S. presidents personified, and the Chamber of Horrors presents yet another assortment of ghouls and goblins. The Hall of Religions recreates the Last Supper, while the Tomb of King Tut paints a detailed portrait of the boy-king's impressive resting place.

Pampanito Submarine — Having sunk six enemy vessels and damaged countless others in World War II, the *U.S.S. Pampanito* submarine now resides at Pier 45 in Fisherman's Wharf. Tours of the *Pampanito* today travel from bow to stern, passing through the torpedo room, bridge and cramped sleeping quarters and creating a vivid feeling of claustrophobia.

Ghirardelli Square — The most attractive commercial complex in Fisherman's Wharf, Ghirardelli Square houses many fine stores, restaurants, galleries and other places to browse. During the mid-nineteenth century, Ghirardelli Square was the site of a wool mill, although the most famous resident and namesake of the square was the Ghirardelli Chocolate Factory. Built by Domenico Ghirardelli in 1900, many of the factory's original, red-brick buildings still remain, as does the landmark sign on the roof and several of the original chocolate-making machines.

Setting a precedent in urban renewal across the country, the factory's conversion was designed by Wurster, Bernardi & Emmons architects and Lawrence Halprin & Associates landscape architects in 1962. The space is a pleasant one through which to meander, with several wide plazas and winding walkways. Street performers entertain throughout the square and, among the

The Ghirardelli Chocolate Factory.

many other interesting sites, the **Ghirardelli Chocolate Factory** still produces luscious candy bars and old-fashioned ice cream.

The Cannery — Following the factory-converting success of Ghirardelli Square, The Cannery building was renovated in 1968 by Joseph Esherick & Associates. Constructed in 1909 by Philip Bush, the original three-story building housed the Del Monte Fruit Company's peach-canning plant. Designed around a sunken courtyard filled with flowers and street performers, the building today contains a comedy club, a movie theater and several galleries, restaurants and shops. Housing a fine collection of civic artifacts and photographs, the **San Francisco Museum** here is perhaps more notable for its ceiling, a thirteenth-century, hand-carved Byzantine mosaic donated by the estate of newspaper magnate William Randolph Hearst.

Ghirardelli Square by night.

Alcatraz Island — The most notorious prison in the country, Alcatraz still grips the imagination. "The Rock," as it was known, was home to the country's most infamous criminals, including Al Capone, Machine Gun Kelly and Robert Stroud, the Birdman of Alcatraz. Unruly inmates who could not be tamed in other facilities were sent to Alcatraz to be broken in. Until this Federal Penitentiary closed in 1963, Alcatraz was deemed escape-proof. Despite fabulous tales of daring flight, there is no evidence to suggests that anyone ever did escape the walls of Alcatraz and survive the strong, frigid, shark-infested currents of the bay.

The island was discovered by a Spanish fleet in 1775 and named Isla de los Alcatraces, Island of the Cormorants. The first lighthouse on the West Coast was built here in 1854, and by the 1860s the island was already being used as a military stockade

Alcatraz Island, known as "The Rock".

for misguided U.S. Army soldiers, Confederate sympathizers and unruly Native American Indians. The cellhouse built by convicts in 1911 was at that time one of the largest reinforced concrete structures in the world. In 1934 Alcatraz Island became a federal prison, but the legend was already born. Since 1972 Alcatraz Island has been a national park.

The dilapidated prison is maintained as a bleak, ominous monument to crime. Ferries to the island leave from Fisherman's Wharf, and tours of the gloomy penitentiary suggest just how miserable a home Alcatraz must have been.

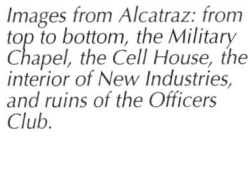

Images from Alcatraz: from top to bottom, the Military Chapel, the Cell House, the interior of New Industries, and ruins of the Officers Club.

Left, guard Keith Dennison in the main cellblock (March 1963).

Below, "Broadway B - C" blocks, the reconstruction of the cells where the famous Escape from Alcatraz began in 1962, and inmates in their cells after lock down (around 1960).

Opposite, clockwise from top left: the library in the penitentiary; spiral staircase in the barbershop; inmates in the cafeteria; Attorney General H. Cummings inspecting the prison guards at the opening of Alcatraz Federal Penitentiary in August, 1934.

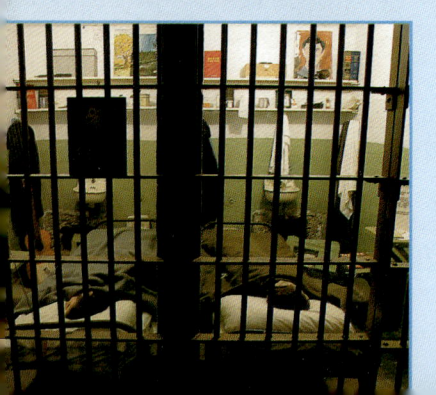

ge 102, left, top to bottom: brothers John and Clarence Anglin and Frank Lee Morris, the three men involved in the "Escape from Alcatraz", June 1962;
age 103: the dummy heads (top) put into their eds to trick the wardens (center), and (bottom) Morris' cell with the enlarged air vent used to escape.

Page 102, right, top to bottom: Miran hompson, Sam Shockley and Clarence Carnes participated in the 1946 "blast out," the bloodiest escape attempt in Alcatraz Federal Penitentiary;
famous guests of Alcatraz was Robert "Birdman" Stroud, interested in bird diseases, and "Machine Gun" Kelly.

101

102

103

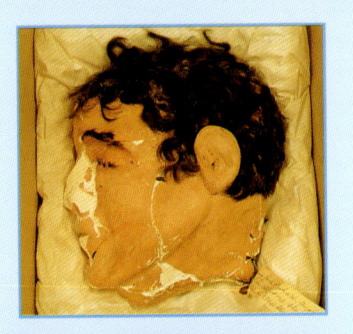

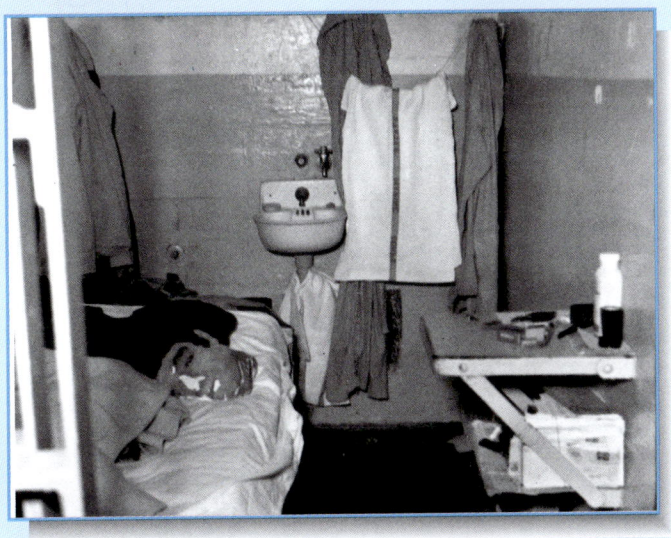

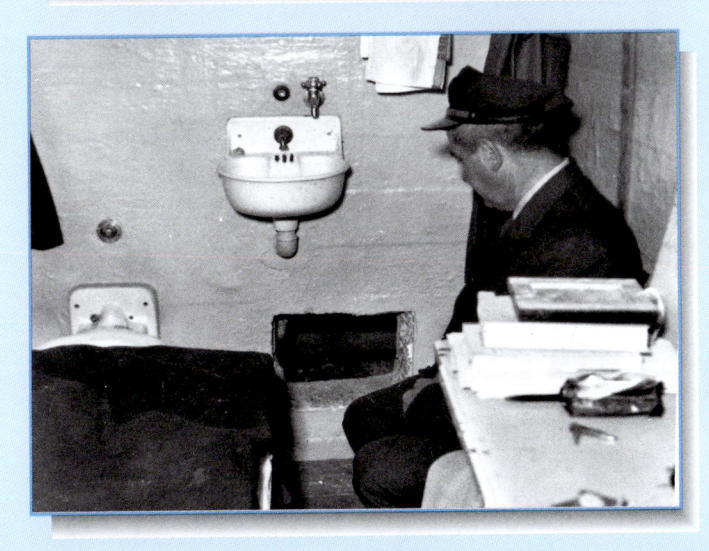

THE EMBARCADERO

Ferry Building — One of the few downtown buildings left standing after the 1906 earthquake, the Ferry Building survived only through the yeomen efforts of fireboats pumping water from the bay. Designed by Arthur Page Brown in 1894 and completed in 1903, the Ferry Building served as the gateway to the city before the advent of the Bay and Golden Gate Bridges in 1937, when ferries were the only practical means of transportation to the city. At one point it was the second busiest gateway in the world: 170 daily ferries ushered in fifty million passengers to the city every year, most of whom were daily commuters from Oakland and Marin County.

At 235 feet tall, the Ferry Building was for many years the tallest structure in the city, a proud beacon for travelers across the bay. Besides the stately clock tower, the building's elegant architecture sports lovely colonnades and internal arcades. The building was modeled after the Moorish belltower of the Giralda Cathedral Tower in Seville, Spain. Remarkably, the building survived the Loma Prieta earthquake of 1989 unscathed, even though the quake did extensive damage to the Embarcadero Freeway that separates the bay-front building from the rest of the city.

After construction of the city's bridges, the building fell largely to disuse. Today only a few ferries come and go each day, and the building is the home of the city's port authority and world trade center. A relic from the D-Day invasion, the **SS Jeremiah O'Brien** anchored along the Em-

The Embarcadero Center.

Justin Herman Plaza: the Vaillancourt Fountain.

barcadero near the Ferry Building is the last of the Liberty Ship launched during World War II. The ship recently returned from a historic voyage to Europe for a celebration commemorating the end of World War II.

Embarcadero Center — The Embarcadero Center is an urban sprawl of landscaped plazas, patios, walkways and bridges that connect four slim, modern towers and cover almost eight square blocks. The center, as well as the four surrounding high-rises, were designed by John Portman and Associates in 1982. Since that time three more buildings have been added. In all, the center houses more than 120 stores, cafés and restaurants that are arranged in a comfortable setting. The center's design is user-friendly, and the outdoor spaces are well conceived.

Vaillancourt Fountain — Designed by Canadian artist Armand Vaillancourt in 1971, the gargantuan Vaillancourt Fountain erupts dramatically from the center of Justin Herman Plaza. This avant-garde structure is considered quite ugly by many, although most admit that it is provocative and intriguing to look at. A convoluted jumble of concrete blocks and metal girders jutting from pools at drastic angles, the fountain spouts grand sheets and columns of water. During frequent times of drought, the fountain unfortunately remains dry.

Victorian Houses
◆ 111

Spreckels Mansion ◆ 109

Japantown, the Peace Pagoda
◆ 112

Filbe
Unic
Valle
Backer
Lyon St

Washington St
Clay St
California St

St. Mary's Cathedral, interior

O'Farrell

University of
San Francisco

Turk Bl

Octagon House
◆ 110

SECTION SIX

PACIFIC HEIGHTS AND CENTRAL NEIGHBORHOODS

St. Mary's Cathedral ◆ 113

PACIFIC HEIGHTS AND VICTORIAN HOUSES

San Francisco's most affluent neighborhood, Pacific Heights features some of the city's loveliest homes, many of which are splendid Victorians built in the wake of the 1906 trembler. The Heights became increasingly blue-blood with the introduction of the cable-car in 1878, when the city's affluent were lured away from the more established enclaves on Nob Hill. Fabulous monstrosities were built as neighbors competed to have the most opulent home. Along Van Ness Avenue especially, houses became quite decadent indeed.

The quake changed all that, of course, but Pacific Heights rose again. The exquisite views and natural beauty of the neighborhood simply could not be matched. Again the mansions were built, designed by such great architects as Willis Polk, Bernard Maybeck, Arthur Brown and George Applegarth. The mansions that grace the tree-lined streets that crest Pacific Heights offer some of the best views in the city of the bay and Golden Gate Bridge. To this day the neighborhood remains the wealthiest area in the city.

Corner of Union Street and Buchanan Street.

Spreckels Mansion, on the north side of Lafayette Park.

*For years the Victorian houses along **Union Street** were some of the city's finest private homes. Today these old Victorians comprises one of the city's most chic commercial thoroughfares. Over 300 boutiques, restaurants, cafés and antique stores line Union Street. **Sacramento Street** and **Upper Fillmore Street** have also developed into major shopping arteries—not quite as trendy as Union Street, but not as touristy either. Here fabulous boutiques and upscale restaurants offer some of the city's finest pleasantries.*

Spreckels Mansion — The single most spectacular house in the city, Spreckels Mansion was built for Adolph and Alma de Bretteville Spreckels in 1912. Adolph was one of many sons of sugar tycoon Claus Spreckels, and Alma—interestingly—was inspiration for the figure of Victory atop the Dewey Monument in Union Square. Their reinforced-concrete mansion, which occupies an entire block on Washington Street, was designed in Beaux Arts splendor by famed city architect George Applegarth. Applegarth would later build the Palace of the Legion of Honor for the Spreckels in the Presidio. Clad in white Utah limestone, the mansion overlooks Lafayette Park and is known as the "Pantheon of the West." It features several large, ornately detailed balconies and French windows. The façade is adorned with elaborate columns and beautiful *putti* statues. The gardens, fittingly, are extensive and well groomed. In 1990, romance novelist Danielle Steel bought the house for $8 million.

Octagon House — Built according to the once-popular superstition that eight-sided houses were lucky, Octagon House was built in 1861. At that time it was one of the city's five eight-sided buildings. The ground floor of Octagon House was altered when the house was moved from its original site across the street, but the upstairs remains the same. The National Society of Colonial Dames, an organization founded in 1891 to preserve the heritage of the country's colonial period, has occupied the house since 1951, when it began an extensive and thoughtful restoration. Since then the building has been converted into a museum that displays decorative arts from the Colonial and Federal periods.

Haas-Lilienthal House — Built in 1886 for wealthy merchant William Haas, the Haas-Lilienthal House is the only fully period-furnished Victorian house in the city open to the public. Designed in the Stick style with ornately carved wooden gables, elaborate ornamentation and a superb Queen Anne circular corner tower, Haas-Lilienthal House is an excellent model of the city's archetypal, nineteenth-century, upper-middle-class Victorian abode. The house was occupied by several generations of the Haas and Lilienthal families until 1972, when it was given to the Foundation for San Francisco's Architectural Heritage and opened as a museum. Inside the house is true to form—the furnishings preserve the time warp, showing just how far tastes have come in the past century.

The Octagon House, built in 1861.

Opposite, Victorian Houses, detail.

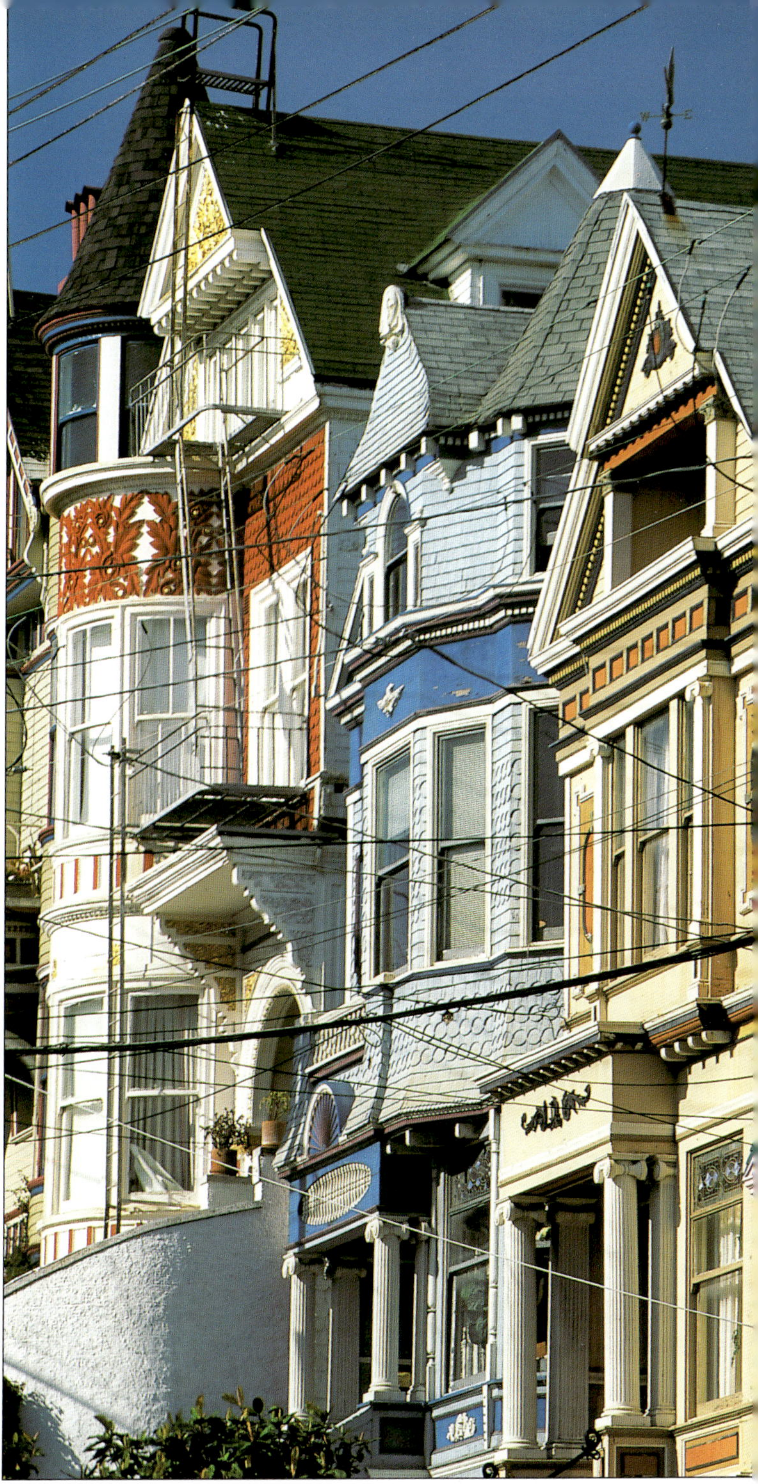

JAPANTOWN

*The majority of Japantown's Japanese population lost their homes during the internment of World War II. Although only four percent of the city's Japanese now live within Japantown's twenty square blocks, the area retains its cultural flavor and many of its ethnic traditions. On weekends the streets of Nihonmachi, as Japantown is called locally, are the site of many age-old rituals and festivals. Many of the properties are decorated with stone lanterns and impressive topiary bushes. The block-long **Buchanan Mall** is landscaped like a traditional Japanese flower garden with fountains designed by renowned sculptor Ruth Asawa.*

Buddhist Church of San Francisco — The Buddhist Church of San Francisco was built by *nisei* architect Gentoko Shimamato in 1938, only a few years before the local Japanese population would be interned in the Utah desert during World War II. During the internment years, the church was maintained by its converted non-Japanese members. The façade of the church is a Roman Baroque design with broken pediments and a dome and finial, which are said to house the relics of the Buddha donated by the King of Siam in 1935. Contrary to its façade, the inside of the church is one of the most peaceful sanctuaries in the city. Up a broad staircase on the second floor, the worship hall is serene and transcendent. The gilded altar is surrounded by beautiful painted screens of peacocks, while the simple wall beams are adorned with ornate gilded panels carved in Kyoto.

Peace Pagoda — The centerpiece of Japan Center, the five-acre shopping and entertainment complex built in 1968, the Peace Pagoda is a 100-foot-tall, five-tiered concrete monument to civic harmony. Rising from the center of Peace Plaza, the pagoda was designed by architect Yoshiro Taniguchi of Tokyo. Although Taniguchi is a re-

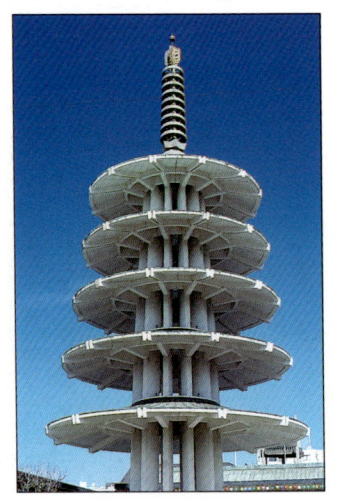

The Peace Pagoda of Japan Center.

spected authority on ancient Japanese architecture, his pagoda looks very modern, like a futuristic radio antenna. Surrounding the plaza are the shopping center's many malls, filled with Japanese shops and restaurants.

St. Mary's Cathedral — Commanding the summit of Cathedral Hill, St. Mary's was built in 1971 and has been one of the city's most distinctive landmarks ever since. Designed by architect Pietro Belluschi and engineer Pier Luigi Nervi, this ultramodern Catholic Cathedral cost $7 million. Its four arching white paraboloids convene to form the 200-foot-high concrete roof in the shape of a Greek cross. Inside, the prevalent feeling is one of vaulting space. A cross-shaped stained-glass window accents the ceiling, while four stained-glass windows rise from floor to ceiling in each main wall, representing the four elements. The cathedral seats 2,500 people around an impressive neo-primitive stone altar backed by a shiny wall of hanging aluminum rods.

The façade and interior of St. Mary's Cathedral, which stands at the top of Cathedral Hill.

M.H. de Young Memorial Museum, *The Bright Side*, by Winslow Homer ◆ 117

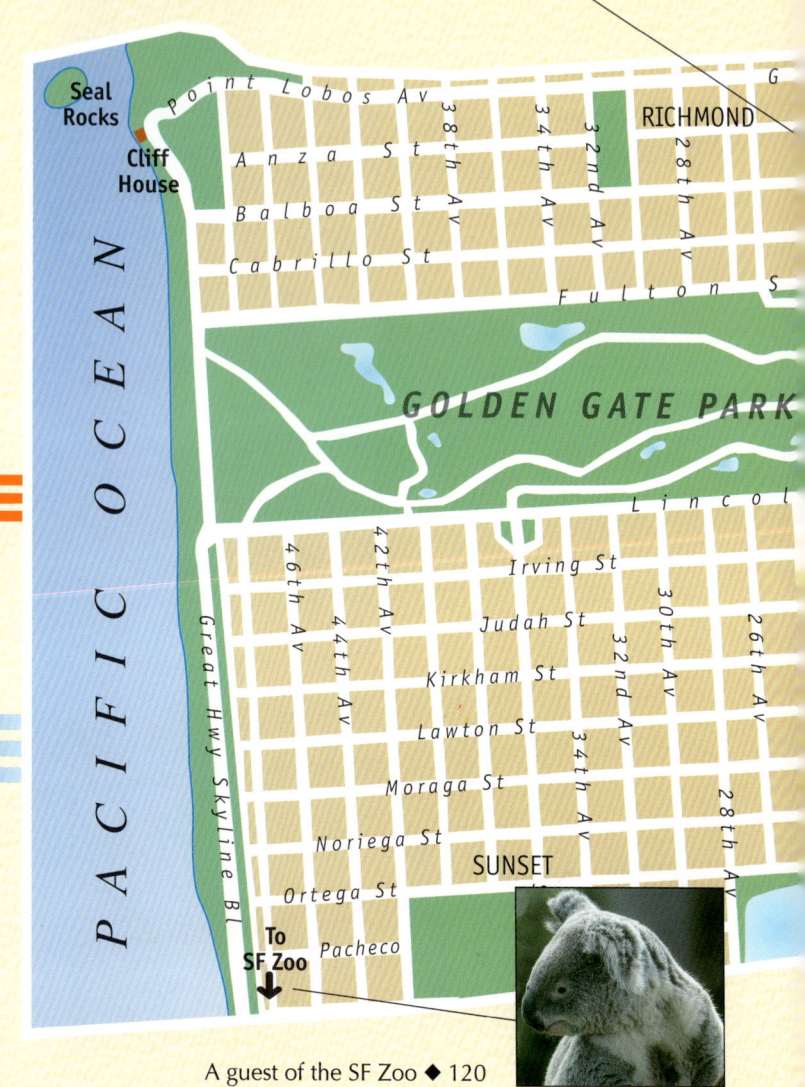

A guest of the SF Zoo ◆ 120

SECTION SEVEN

GOLDEN GATE PARK AND THE WEST

A Diego Rivera's painting, M.H. de Young Memorial Museum ◆ 117

Conservatory of Flowers ◆ 118

Japanese Tea Garden ◆ 119

GOLDEN GATE PARK

Once an embarrassment to the city, a stretch of briny, infertile land that nay-sayers believed impregnable to cultivation, Golden Gate Park is today a paragon of urban landscape architecture. When invited by the city to offer his expertise, Frederick Law Olmstead, architect of New York City's Central Park, deemed the Golden Gate Park project impossible. William Hammond Hall, on the other hand, had a vision. He designed the park in 1866, and work began in 1871 with the creation of the Panhandle.

Hall's original plan aside, the man most responsible for the park's triumphant success was John McLaren, the young Scotsman who became superintendent of gardening in 1890. For over fifty years until his death in 1943, McLaren cultivated the land, planting first grass and small shrubs to solidify the ground and then larger bushes and trees. Over his career, he was responsible for planting over a million trees, many of which grew up to eighty feet tall. McLaren's statue stands at the entrance to **Rhododendron Dell**. Today the park indeed feels far removed from the strains and stresses of the city. Paved walkways meander through the landscape of flowers, meadows, lakes, hills and forests. The **Strybing Arboretum** alone includes over 6,000 species of trees, plants and shrubs, some indigenous to northern California and others imported. Plants are selected for their taste, touch and smell, with one garden dedicated to the olfactory senses alone. The **Shakespeare Garden**, on the other hand, features only those flowers and plants alluded to in the Great Bard's sonnets and plays, with the relevant quotes written on plaques set in a wall at the back of the garden. Marked by the large Dutch windmill built in the park's northwest corner in 1903, the **Queen Wilhelmina Tulip Garden** features a colorful array of tulips that bloom each spring. A much woolier experience, the thirty-five-acre **Buffalo Paddock** was opened in 1892 and is currently home to fourteen shaggy American bison, the largest animals on North American soil.

In addition to the flower gardens and sanctuaries, there are countless playing fields as well as a host of highly respected museums and cultural centers.

Opposite, M. H. de Young Memorial Museum, clockwise from top left:
Two Women and a Child, by Diego Rivera, 1926;
Caroline de Bassano, Marquise d'Espeuilles, by John Singer Sargent, 1884;
Oranges in Tissue Paper, by William J. McCloskey, ca. 1890;
Job Lot Cheap, 1892, John Frederick Peto;
The Bright Side, by Winslow Homer, 1865;
The Ironworkers' Noontime, by Thomas Pollock Anshutz, 1880.

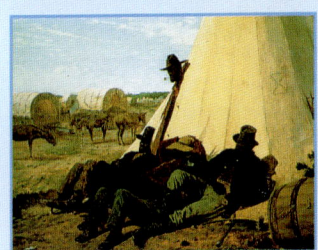

M.H. de Young Memorial Museum — The idea for the museum was conceived by *San Francisco Chronicle* publisher Michael de Young, who organized the California Midwinter International Exposition of 1894 on 200 acres in the park. De Young promoted the fair far and wide and used the proceeds to fund a permanent art museum for the city.

The museum's galleries hold the city's main collection of American art, which includes paintings, sculptures and decorative arts from Colonial times to the twentieth century. Some of the American masters on display are William Harnett, John Peto, Alexander Pope, John Singleton Copley, James Peale, Mary Cassatt, John Singer Sargent and James McNeill Whistler. Modern American greats include the works of Wayne Thiebaud, Georgia O'Keeffe, Grant Wood and Reginald Marsh.

A brand new De Young Memorial Museum is planned to be built on the same site as the original building (1919), and it will be ready by the year 2005.

Asian Art Museum — The Asian Art Museum was opened in 1966 after Avery Brundage donated his renowned Asian art collection to the city. An engineering mogul known better as the long-serving president of the International Olympic Committee, Brundage amassed his collection over a lifetime. He chose to donate it to San Francisco because of the city's long-standing social links with Asia.

Today the collection totals more than 12,000 pieces, making the museum the largest of its kind in the U.S. Artworks range from paintings and sculptures to all imaginable decorative arts. The exhibit includes works from Korea and China, the focus of Brundage's passionate collecting, as well as from the rest of Asia.

Housed for several years in the De Young Museum's west wing, the Museum is planned to be moved to its new Civic Center home in 2002.

California Academy of Sciences — The West's oldest scientific institution, the California Academy of Sciences was founded on Market Street in 1853. After the original Academy was destroyed by fire in 1906, it opened its doors in the park in 1916. The Academy's grandiose building faces the M.H. de Young Museum and includes museums, exhibition halls, a planetarium and an aquarium. The Academy's **Natural History Museum** includes a remarkable Gem and Mineral Hall as well as the Hohfeld Earth and Space Hall, which has an exhibit that simulates the tremors of the city's two famous quakes. The Wild California and African Safari galleries show the diversity of both habitat's wildlife. The Discovery Room for Children presents many interesting hands-on exhibitions that aren't just for kids.

Under a sixty-five-foot-high dome, the **Morrison Planetarium** is northern California's largest indoor solar system. The dome serves as backdrop for highly entertaining sky shows. The Planetarium's Laserium features a choreographed, one-hour laser show accompanied by throbbing rock music. Perhaps the most impressive section in the Academy, the **Steinhart Aquarium** displays the world's most diverse collection of sea creatures, including over 14,000 species of fish. There is also a simulated swamp that features a host of creepy reptiles and amphibians such as alligators, lizards and turtles. Another exhibit has dolphins, seals and penguins playing to the crowd. The most spectacular display, however, is the 100,000-gallon Fish Roundabout, a glass-enclosed tunnel surrounded on all sides by thousands of fish, including sharks and sting rays.

The Conservatory of Flowers — Constructed by Lord and Burnham in 1878, the Conservatory is the oldest building in the park. Inspired by the Palm House at Kew Gardens in London, the structure's frame was actually built in Dublin and shipped around Cape Horn. Eccentric millionaire

James Lick commissioned the ornate glasshouse building—which miraculously survived two major earthquake—but did not live to see it constructed. The Conservatory displays a collection of tropical plants and orchids and has special flower shows each season. The stunning gardens surrounding the Conservatory are filled with flowers and groves of camellias, fuchsias and dahlias.
At the moment the building is under renovation because of the damages caused by recent years' rough weather and it is scheduled to reopen in the near future.

Japanese Tea Garden — The Japanese Tea Garden is one of the crown jewels of Golden Gate Park. Built by art dealer George Marsh for the California Midwinter International Exposition of 1894, the garden was preserved by park overlord John McLaren after the exposition ended. Prominent gardeners, the Hagiwara family took charge of the garden until World War II, when they were sent to internment camps along with 110,000 other Japanese-Americans living in northern California. Today the garden is a perfect blend of nature and architecture. Bridges, footpaths, statuary and gates meld seamlessly into the natural landscape of trees, flowers and streams. When the cherry trees bloom in April, the garden is ablaze in soft pinks and

The Conservatory of Flowers and, right, the Japanese Tea Garden.

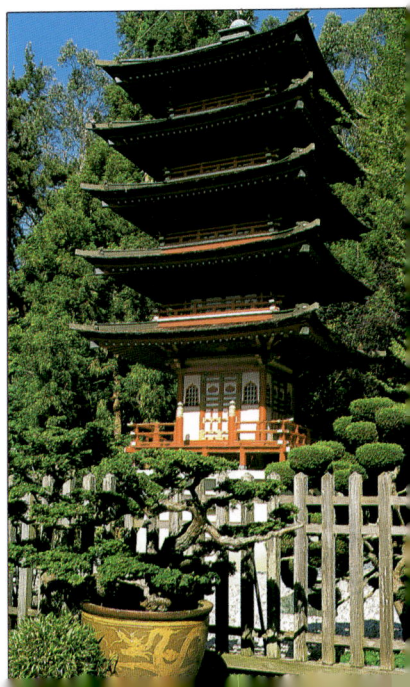

white. Cast in Japan in 1790, an eleven-foot bronze **Buddha**—the largest outside of Asia—sits at the top of a set of garden stairs. Another impressive monument, the **Shinto Pagoda** is a five-tiered wooden shrine. Along with its reflection in the pond below, the steeply arched **Wishing Bridge** forms a perfect circle when viewed from above.

San Francisco Zoo — Opened in 1929, the San Francisco Zoo covers sixty-five acres of parkland in the city's far southwest corner, between the Pacific Ocean and Lake Merced. The zoo has over 1,000 species of birds and mammals, thirty of which are considered to be endangered. Natural habitats are gradually replacing the concrete cages with metal bars. A good example of the trend is Gorilla World, one of the world's largest naturalistic zoo settings. Koala Crossing is another highlight, designed to be like the Australian outback. The Lion House is the site of bloody carnage most days at 2PM, when the big cats are fed. The innovative Primate Discovery Center features interactive computer programs that describe the monkeys and apes. The Children's Zoo features a host of animals that like to be petted.

The koala, a guest of the San Francisco Zoo.

OTHER

San Francisco-Oakland Bay Bridge — The longest steel structure in the world, the Bay Bridge was also one of the costliest ever built. The dream team of engineers Charles Purcell, Charles Andrew, Glenn Woodruff and architect Timothy Pfleuger designed the project during the depths of the Great Depression. The 8.25-mile structure is actually made up of two bridges, each 2,310 feet long, that are joined in the middle by a tunnel through Yerba Buena Island, which at the time was the world's widest. The project took three years to build and was finally opened in 1936. The New Deal Reconstruction Finance Corporation footed the $70 million bill.
4.25 miles of the bridge hover over the Bay, 190 feet below. These sections are supported by massive piers that are, quite literally, without peers. The bridge itself swallowed eighteen percent of the steel produced in the United States in 1933. The two-level bridge is a complex structure that employs a cantilever design on the Oakland side and a doudle-suspension design on the San Francisco side. While the lower deck was originally designed to transport electric trains, today each level has five car lanes that usher 250,000 motorists on their way every day.

Pacific Bell Park on Opening Day.

During the 1989 Loma Prieta earthquake, a frightening accident occurred when the bridge's upper deck collapsed onto the lower, killing one person. Amazingly, a herculean construction effort kept the bridge closed for only one month.

3-Com and Pacific Bell Parks — The famous city's field Candlestick Park, now officially called 3-Com Park, is home of the five-time Super Bowl champion 49ers. Three miles south of San Francisco via US 101, 3-Com seats over 60,000 people. The "Stick," as it is known, was the first stadium to be made entirely of reinforced concrete. Built in 1960 by John S. Bolles and Associates, the stadium sits right on the edge of the Bay, a proximity that makes playing conditions notoriously cool and windy.
Pacific Bell Park, home of the San Francisco Giants, opened to rave reviews in April of 2000. The intimate baseball park situated on San Francisco Bay in the South of Market area, seats approximately 41,000 fans. A well struck ball hit to right field can actually clear the stadium and land in the bay waters, now called Mc Covey Cove.

Cow Palace — The Cow Palace is an all-purpose auditorium that was first used to host livestock shows. This large hall can seat up to 14,300 people, and it counts among its greatest moments a concert by the Beatles in the late 1960s.

Yerba Buena Island — Yerba Buena Island is known primarily as the midpoint tunnel of the Bay Bridge. Its history far predates construction of the bridge, however, and even the advent of the city itself. Indians once used the island as a fishing station. The remains of a village have been unearthed on the island, along with buried pirate treasure, parts of a swamped Spanish warship and the graves of various waves of soldiers, pioneers and shepherds. The island got its name, "Good Herb," from the tasty wild mint that grew there. Today the island is a Coast Guard Reservation and Naval Training Station.

Treasure Island — After having constructed two of the world's largest bridges in the same year, San Francisco saw fit to build yet another structure to commemorate its labors. Treasure Island was created to host the Golden Gate International Exposition of 1939-40. The 400-acre man-made island was funded by a $3-million grant from the WPA, which financed government building projects during the Depression. Only a hop and a skip from the Bay Bridge, the island was deemed an unsuitable location for the San Francisco airport and 1941 became a U.S. Navy base instead. The **Treasure Island Museum** has exhibits on the history of the Marine Corps, the creation of the island and the innovations unveiled at the world's fair.

EASY TRIPS FROM SAN FRANCISCO

San Francisco serves well as a hub for day and weekend forays into northern California. San Francisco's proximity to countless natural wonders is part of the city's irresistible charm. Before leaving the city though, consider undertaking the **49 Mile Scenic Drive**, which gives a wonderful overview of the city. The drive cuts along the coast and through the hills, revealing some of the city's finest sights. The course is well marked with blue-and-white sea gull signs and takes about a day to complete. There are plenty of places to stop along the way to admire the natural and architectural landscape.

To the north of the city, the sleepy, hillside town of **Sausalito** is a great place to escape for a day and walk along the shops and galleries and take lunch overlooking San Francisco on the other side of the bay. A similar day can be passed on the peninsula of **Tiburon** or on **Angel Island**, both just a ferry ride away from Fisherman's Wharf. With more than sixty-eight square miles, the **Golden Gate National Recreation Area** encompasses several parks within San Francisco and spills into the Marin Headlands, a wilderness area across the Golden Gate Bridge where some good hiking can be had. A bit further from the city, a hike through the 800-year-old redwoods of **Muir Woods** can also be a treat. Nearby, **Stinson Beach** is a three-mile stretch of white sand that is one of the Bay Area's most popular swimming spots. About thirty

Top, Sausalito. Right, Muir Woods with the 800-year-old redwoods.

miles north on the coast is **Bodega Bay**, a quaint, rustic fishing village that is appealing simply for its relaxed ambience. Sporting a similar milieu still further up the coast, the former logging town of **Mendocino** is perhaps even more transcendent—a vision from the mid-1800s—especially when the fog shrouds this coastal bluff. Inland, about an hour's drive north of San Francisco, lies the wine country of the **Sonoma and Napa Valleys**, home to some of the world's finest vineyards. Visitors can stop for lunch and a tour of most wineries throughout the area.

To the South of San Francisco lies the sprawling campus of **Stanford University**, founded by railroad giant Leland Stanford in 1892 and now one of the world's greatest institutions of higher learning. Many of Stanford's finest students go on to work in **Silicon Valley** nearby, birthplace of the technological and computer revolution. Northern California's answer to Disneyland, **Great America** has amusement rides for the lion-hearted and yellow-bellied alike. Or if sitting on a beautiful beach watching surfers shred waves sounds like more fun, **Santa Cruz** is the place to go. Down the Monterey Peninsula are the picturesque towns of **Monterey** and **Carmel**, known for their beautiful homes and the scenic 17-Mile Drive that links them. Further south is **Big Sur**, an awe-inspiring stretch of cliffs along the coast.

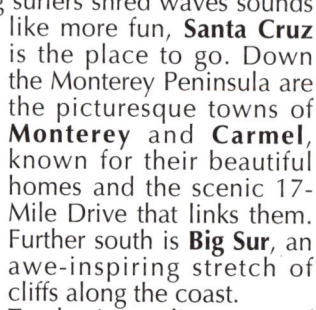

To the immediate east of San Francisco, right over the Bay Bridge in fact, lie the cities of **Oakland** and **Berkeley**. Renowned as a hotbed of liberal politics, **the University of California at Berkeley** was the focus of the counterculture revo-

The Wine Country, north of San Francisco.

Californians are proud of their vineyards, which are among the best in the world.

The Orange Poppy, California's state flower, thrives in the gardens of the many of the vineyards.

lution in the 1960s. With animals approaching so close you can feel their breath—not to mention smell it—**Six Flags Marine World** in Vallejo is any animal lovers dream come true. The wildlife is pretty impressive in **Yosemite National Park** as well, where Vernal Fall, Half Dome and the Grizzly Giant sequoia are sure to astound. One of the most beautiful bodies of water in the world, **Lake Tahoe** is surrounded by forested peaks that are as great for skiing in the winter as they are for cavorting in the summer. The pioneering spirit lives on in **Gold Country**, a series of small towns near the Sierra Nevada mountains that grew up during the Gold Rush and still retain their nineteenth-century charm.

Yosemite National Park, the "Half Dome" monolith.

WINE

California wine has been coming of age for well over a century, since Hungarian émigré and adventurer Count Agoston Haraszthy brought hundreds of **vitis vinifera** cuttings from Europe in 1856 and planted them near the town of Sonoma. While the personal success of the pioneer's enterprise was limited, the reverberations of his initial efforts have been immense. Today, after more than a century of ups and downs, the quality and success of California wine is undisputed. The winemaking revival starting in the Napa Valley three decades ago, and then spreading to the Sonoma Valley and northward to Mendocino County, has attracted many newcomers into the business, from rat-race dropouts to multinational corporations and at least one famous film director.

At the same time, some of Europe's most renowned wine producers have added a California label and set up operations in the Wine Country.

There are also numerous small, family-run outfits, some of which produce superb if not easy to find vintages.

INDEX

Alamo Square 35
Alcatraz Island 98
Ansel Adams Center for Photography .67
Asian Art Museum 118
Baker Beach 83
Balmy Street Murals 72
Bank of Canton 42
Basic Brown Bears ..73
Bill Graham Civic Auditorium 35
Buddhist Church of San Francisco 112
Cable Car Museum .59
California Academy of Sciences...............118
California Palace of the Legion of Honor 82
Cannery (The) 97
Castro (The) 77
Chestnut Street 90
China Beach 83
Chinatown 38
Chinatown Gateway 40
Chinese Historical Society of America Museum 42
City Hall 31
Civic Center 30
Cliff House 82
Coit Tower 50
Conservatory of Flowers 118
Cow Palace 122
Crocker Galleria 16
Downtown 7
Embarcadero Center 105
Esplanade 63
Fairmont Hotel 54
Ferry Building 104
Filbert and Greenwich Steps 52
Financial District 18
Fisherman's Wharf ..92
Fort Mason 91
Fort Point 83
Galeria de la Raza ..72
Ghirardelli Square ..96
Golden Gate Bridge 84
Golden Gate Park .116
Grace Cathedral 55
Haas-Lilienthal House 110
Haight (The) 76
Haight-Ashbury 77
Huntington Hotel 56
Jackson Square Historical District .26
Japanese Tea Garden 119
Japantown 112

Levi Strauss & Company 72
Lombard Street 52
Louise M. Davies Symphony Hall 33
Maiden Lane 11
Marina (The)........... 89
Marina Green 89
Mark Hopkins International Hotel 56
Merchant's Exchange Building 24
M.H. de Young Memorial Museum 117
Mission (The) 69
Mission Dolores...... 70
Moscone Convention Center 62
New San Francisco Main Public Library 34
Nob Hill 54
Noe Valley 76
North Beach 44
Northern Waterfront 91
Octagon House 110
Old Mint Museum ..67
Outdoor Murals 71
Pacific Bell Park ...122
Pacific Coast Stock Exchange 28
Pacific Heights 108
Pacific-Union Club .57
Palace of Fine Arts ..89
Pampanito Submarine 96
Peace Pagoda 112
Pet Cemetery 81
Pier 39 93
Portsmouth Square ..40
Potrero Hill District .73
Powell Street Cable-Car Turnaround ...12
Presidio (The) 80
Presidio Army Museum 81
Ritz Carlton Hotel ...57
Russian Hill 52
Saints Peter and Paul Roman Catholic Church 47
San Francisco Art Institute 53
San Francisco Museum of Modern Art 64
San Francisco National Maritime Museum 94
San Francisco Shopping Centre 16
San Francisco Zoo 120
San Francisco-Oakland Bay Bridge 121
Shopping 16
Showplace Square ..73

Sony Metreon 63
South of Market 62
South Park 68
Spreckels Mansion 109
St. Mary's Cathedral 113
Stouffer Stanford Court Hotel.....................58
Telegraph Hill 49
Theatres 15
Theater District 15
3-COM Park 122
Tien Hau Temple 43
Transamerica Pyramid 22
Treasure Island 122
24th Street 71
29 Russell Street 53
Twin Peaks 75
Union Square 8
Vaillancourt Fountain 105
Victorian Houses ..108
War Memorial Opera House 32
Washington Square .46
Waterfront (The) 79
Wax Museum 96
Wells Fargo Bank History Museum ...24
Yerba Buena Gardens 63
Yerba Buena Island 122

EASY TRIPS FROM SAN FRANCISCO..123
Angel Island 123
Berkeley 124
Big Sur 124
Bodega Bay 124
Carmel 124
49 Mile Scenic Drive 123
Gold Country 125
Golden Gate National Recreation Area 123
Great America 124
Lake Tahoe 125
Mendocino 125
Monterey 123
Muir Woods 123
Oakland 124
Santa Cruz 124
Sausalito 123
Silicon Valley 124
Six Flags Marine World 125
Sonoma and Napa Valleys 124
Stanford University 124
Stinson Beach 123
Tiburon 123
University of California at Berkeley 124
Yosemite National Park 125